welcome

Knitting pullovers, cardigans, jackets, and shells to wear and to give is a tactile and rewarding experience that keeps getting better and better. Today's yarns are softer and more colorful than ever, the variety of patterns provides endless possibilities for creating wearables, and caring for knitted wear complies with our wishes to keep it simple. In addition, the act of knitting is relaxing while fulfilling an innate desire to create beauty—beauty that satisfies in yet another way because you'll be wearing what you've created. With so few tools and materials required, you'll discover that packing up and toting projects is convenient. Knitting can creatively fill travel or waiting times and is enhanced when you join other knitters as a member of a club or informal group.

Whether you knit in your easy chair, in a waiting room, on the road, or with a group, we're confident that our collection in *Knitted Sweaters for Her* is so versatile and appealing that you'll be eager to reach immediately for your needles. Once you choose a project, it's easy to get started, following the thorough instructions we've provided, complete materials lists, and abundant illustrations—all to ensure success with every sweater you knit.

From beginning projects, such as the Basic Sweater on *page 2* and My First Cardigan on *page 4* to the more demanding Diamond Lace Twin Set on *page 36,* you'll be joining the ranks of knitters who have already discovered the joys of this craft. We wish you beautiful days with abundant yarns and a wide assortment of knitting needles.

happy knitting!

Page 22

Page 36

contents

Pair it with jeans or your favorite wool skirt. Add a scarf, a big shawl, or cinch a belt around the waist. Or leave it plain! Anyway you wear it, this pullover is a wardrobe classic.

DESIGN: ANN E. SMITH

SKILL LEVEL: EASY

Now that you're comfortable with knitting basics, it's time to work on something that requires a bit of shaping—the kind you'll find on this easy-going number.

basic SWEATER

SIZES

XS (S, M, L, XL, XXL)

Shown in Size S with changes for larger sizes shown in parentheses. When only one number is given, it applies to all sizes.

Note: For ease in working, circle all numbers pertaining to your size before you begin the pattern.

FINISHED MEASUREMENTS

Chest = 32 (36, 40, 44, 48, 52)"
Length = 22 (22½, 23, 23½, 24, 24½)"

YARN

Lion Brand Homespun (Art. 790); 98% acrylic/2% polyester; 185 yds. (169 m); bulky weight
• 3 (4, 4, 5, 5, 5) skeins #336 Barrington

NEEDLES & EXTRAS

• Size 10 (6 mm) knitting needles OR SIZE NEEDED TO OBTAIN GAUGE
• Size 8 (5 mm) knitting needles
• Yarn needle

GAUGE

In St st (k on RS, p on WS) with larger needles, 14 sts and 20 rows = 4" (10 cm). TAKE TIME TO CHECK YOUR GAUGE.

INSTRUCTIONS
BACK

Beg at the lower edge with smaller needles, cast on 56 (63, 70, 77, 84, 91) sts. K 6 rows for Garter st (knit every row) band. Change to larger needles. Beg with a p row, work in St st (k 1 row, p 1 row) until piece measures approx 15" from beg, ending with a p row. At beg of next 2 rows, bind off 4 sts. Continue in St st on rem 48 (55, 62, 69, 76, 83) sts to approx 21 (21½, 22, 22½, 23, 23½)" from beg, ending with a k row.

Shape neckband:
Row 1 (WS): P11 (14, 17, 20, 23, 26) sts, k26 (27, 28, 29, 30, 31) sts, p to end.
Row 2 and each following RS row: Knit.
Row 3: P10 (13, 16, 19, 22, 25), k28 (29, 30, 31, 32, 33), p to end.
Row 5: P9 (12, 15, 18, 21, 24), k30 (31, 32, 33, 34, 35), p to end. With the RS facing, bind off kwise and loosely.

FRONT

Work as for Back until piece measures approx 19 (19½, 20, 20½, 21, 21½)" from beg, ending with a k row. Shape neckband as for Back (Rows 1–5 above).

Shape neck: On next RS row, k13 (16, 19, 22, 25, 28) sts, bind off center 22 (23, 24, 25, 26, 27) sts; k to end.

Right Shoulder: P9 (12, 15, 18, 21, 24), k4. K across next row. Rep last 2 rows until piece measures approx 22 (22½, 23, 23½, 24, 24½)" from beg, ending with WS row. Bind off kwise and loosely.

Left Shoulder: With WS facing, join yarn at neck edge. K4, p to end. K across next row. Rep last 2 rows to same length as Right Shoulder, ending with WS row. Bind off kwise and loosely.

SLEEVES (MAKE 2)

Beg at lower edge with smaller needles, cast on 31 (32, 34, 35, 37, 38) sts. K 6 rows for border. Change to larger needles and p across next row. Working in St st, inc 1 st (k in front and in back of same st) each edge now. Then inc 1 st each edge every 10th row 3 (2, 0, 0, 0, 0) times, every 8th row 5 (7, 8, 5, 2, 1) times, and every 6th row 0 (0, 2, 6, 10, 12) times. Work even on the 49 (52, 56, 59, 63, 66) sts to approx 18½ (19, 19½, 19½, 19½, 20)" from beg, ending with a p row. Bind off kwise and loosely.

FINISHING

Join shoulder seams. Set in sleeves, sewing bound-off sts on body to sides of upper sleeves. Join underarm and side seams. Weave in loose ends.

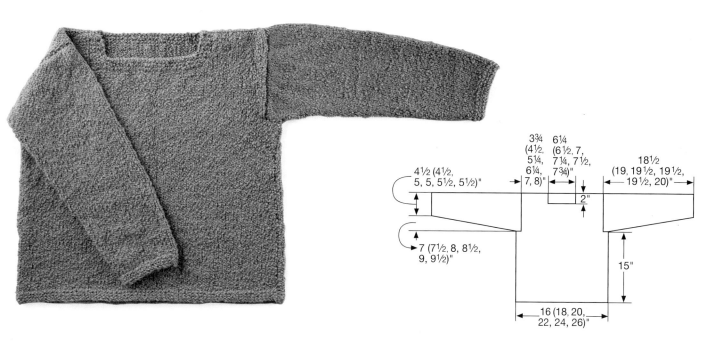

my first
CARDIGAN

Follow these instructions to knit your first cardigan. The steps and tips will give you confidence to complete a project that you'll be proud to wear or give as a gift.

DESIGN: KATHY ZIMMERMAN

SKILL LEVEL: INTERMEDIATE +

You're ready to knit a cardigan after you've completed a pullover sweater or two. This cardigan offers wardrobe versatility and provides opportunities to advance your knitting skills.

Although instructions for the back and sleeves on a cardigan are similar to those of a pullover, the two fronts may present challenges. Following the standard format, begin knitting the back.

Back

Work from the bottom up as instructed until you reach the armhole shaping. Begin the right armhole bind-off on a right side row and the left armhole bind-off on a wrong side row. In subsequent rows, use left-slant decreases along the right armhole (see the Decrease Tips, page 43) and right-slant decreases along the left armhole. Neckline shaping usually has right-slant decreases along the right neckline edge and left-slant decreases along the left. Although these decrease methods are not hard and fast rules, they can be applied successfully in most cases. If the pattern you follow has specific instructions for increasing and decreasing, follow those instructions.

Back neck stitches are either bound off or slipped onto a stitch holder and picked up later to finish the neckline. Binding off the back neck stitches stabilizes the garment and helps prevent the fabric from stretching—this is especially true when working with dense nonelastic fibers or heavyweight yarns.

Cardigan Fronts

Because one front has detailed instructions and the second doesn't, this phrase may puzzle you: "Work as for left (or right) front, reversing all shaping." Here are some tips you'll find helpful.

Left Front

The center left front edge is at the end of right side rows (beginning of wrong side rows). The armhole bind-off begins on a right side row, and left-slant decreases complete the armhole shaping. The neckline bind-off begins on a wrong side row followed by right-slant decreases.

Right Front

The center right front edge is at the beginning of right side rows (end of wrong side rows). The armhole bind-off begins on a wrong side row, and right-slant decreases complete the shaping. The neckline bind-off begins on a right side row followed by left-slant decreases.

Sleeves

These are made the same as pullover sleeves. Work bind-off rows loosely to avoid distortion and pulling. Check row gauge frequently because the sleeve weight can easily change the gauge.

Picking Up Stitches

Before picking up stitches or seaming, wet or dampen the garment pieces, block to desired measurements, and allow the pieces to dry. The edges lie flatter, and it's easier to work the stitches and rows.

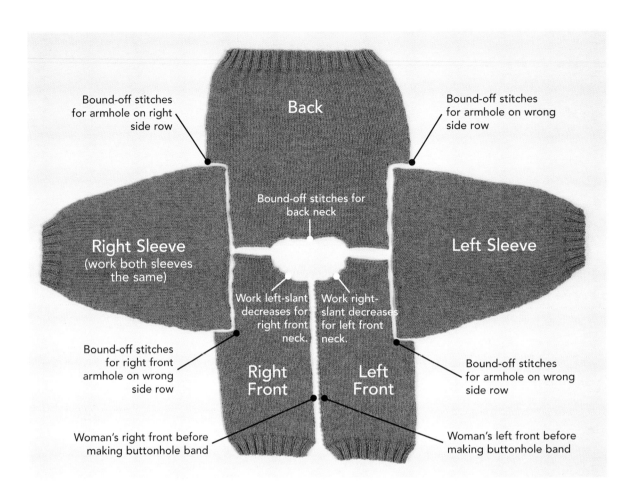

Bound-off stitches for armhole on right side row

Bound-off stitches for armhole on wrong side row

Back

Bound-off stitches for back neck

Right Sleeve (work both sleeves the same)

Left Sleeve

Work left-slant decreases for right front neck.

Work right-slant decreases for left front neck.

Bound-off stitches for right front armhole on wrong side row

Right Front

Left Front

Bound-off stitches for armhole on wrong side row

Woman's right front before making buttonhole band

Woman's left front before making buttonhole band

Pick up stitches with the right (outer) side facing you, using either a crochet hook or a knitting needle. Use a smaller size needle than planned for the border pattern, changing needles when the border begins. Join the yarn and knit or purl the picked-up stitch. Across horizontal edges, pick up each "live," or bound-off, stitch in the first row below the bind-off row. Along vertical edges, such as an armhole or the front band, pick up the whole stitch unless directed otherwise, working 2 stitches every 3 rows, or 3 stitches every 4 rows. For diagonal or curved pickup, as in a crew or V neckline, pick up stitches one for one until the edge becomes vertical, and then use the same pickup ratio planned for the front edges.

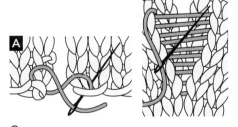

Seams

Invisible Vertical Seam (sometimes called ladder or mattress stitch)—a good seam for sides and sleeves. Thread a yarn needle with the garment yarn, or an appropriate seaming thread if the main yarn is unsuitable for sewing. Working with right sides up, anchor the two cast-on edges together by making a "figure 8" with the yarn. (See illustration A, *above left*.) Begin the seam by * inserting the yarn needle under the running bar between the first two stitches on one piece. Pull the yarn through, and repeat from * on the other piece of the work. Alternate back and forth

between each piece. Insert the yarn needle under one bar, working row by row, or under two running bars. The seam tension should match your row gauge, and the finished seam should withstand the garment use. There are several variations of this technique. (See illustration B, *left*, for one variety.)

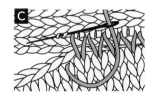

Invisible Vertical-to-Horizontal Seam— joins bound-off stitches to rows and is good for attaching sleeves to armholes. With a threaded yarn needle, insert the needle under the first leg of the first stitch beneath the bound-off edge (coming up through the stitch center). * Insert the needle under one horizontal bar between the first and second stitches of the sweater body; then insert the needle under the next two legs of the stitches beneath the bound-off edge.* Repeat between the *s until the pieces are joined. Because this method attaches rows to stitches (differing gauges), you will occasionally need to work under two horizontal bars to keep the pieces even. (See illustration C, *opposite right*.)

Shoulder Seams

Garments with sleeves require stable shoulder seams capable of supporting sleeve weight. To determine which seaming method to use, consider garment size, yarn weight, and stitch pattern.

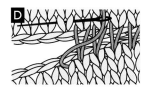

Invisible Horizontal—Lay both the back and front sections flat and right side up, with corresponding stitches aligned. Join the yarn to the right edge; with the threaded needle and working in the first row under the bind-off row, insert the needle under one leg of the first stitch on the front piece (coming up through the stitch center); * then insert the needle under both legs of the first stitch adjacent to the bind-off on the back piece. Insert the needle under the next two legs of the front stitch.* Repeat between *s across the shoulder. (See illustration D, *above*.)

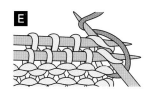

3-Needle Bind-Off—binds off and joins two pieces together in one action. Use a smaller size knitting needle to hold the shoulder stitches, and work the bind-off with the body size knitting needle. Slip the stitches from one back shoulder onto a knitting needle; then slip the corresponding front shoulder stitches onto another knitting needle. Place the work right sides together, with both needles aligned and the tips pointing to the right.

Join the yarn at the right edge, and insert the third knitting needle into the first stitch on both needles. Knit these two stitches together (one stitch on the third needle); * knit the next two stitches together (two stitches on the third needle). Bind off one stitch from the third needle (one stitch remains on the third needle)*. Repeat between *s until one stitch remains on the right needle. Cut the yarn; then thread the yarn tail through the stitch and pull to secure. (See illustration E, *below left*.)

Sleeves to Armholes

When attaching sleeves to the body, sew the shoulder seams first. Fold the sleeve in half lengthwise, and place a stitch marker at the center top of the sleeve. On each side of center, place another stitch marker halfway down the sleeve. Place corresponding stitch markers along the body armhole halfway between the shoulder seam and the armhole bind-off. Matching all markers, pin the pieces together. Thread the needle with yarn and attach the sleeves to the body.

Front Bands

Front bands are made horizontally or vertically; instructions usually indicate which band to make.

The horizontal band is worked at right angles to the main body—joining stitches to rows. Pick up the required stitches along the front edge and work back and forth in the pattern for the desired width and then bind off. Although instructions usually specify the number of stitches to pick up, if your gauge varies or you've altered the pattern, those numbers won't work. Before you start a horizontal band, work the border pattern along the edge of your gauge swatch to help you determine the best pickup ratio.

A vertical band is normally worked in the same direction as the garment. The following are two easy methods: (1) Make the bands separately and stitch them to the fronts during the finishing. (2) Cast on the band stitches with the front ribbing; when the ribbing is finished, place the band stitches on holders. To finish either kind of band, add one stitch for seaming, complete the band, and sew it to the front.

Button and Buttonhole Placement

The first and last buttons are usually placed ½ to 1 inch from the top and lower edges, and the remaining buttons are spaced equally apart between them. You may need to modify the spacing or add an extra button or two to keep the bands from gaping open. A woman's cardigan has buttons on the left band and buttonholes on the right. A man's cardigan has buttons on the right band and buttonholes on the left.

Whenever possible, make the button band before the buttonhole band. Position the upper and lower buttons, and place the other buttons, evenly spaced, where you want them. Count the rows or stitches between the top and bottom buttons. For a vertical band, divide the number of rows by the number of spaces between buttons. For a horizontal band, divide the number of stitches by the number of spaces between the buttons. If the numbers don't divide evenly, use the extra rows or stitches before the first button or after the last one. A tape measure isn't a good tool for this job—count the rows or stitches instead. Mark each button position with a small pin or colored thread.

BUTTONHOLES—Align each buttonhole placement with its corresponding button marker. Try to start and end the buttonholes where they are less visible, usually the purl stitch in ribbing. Knitting stretches, so make the buttonholes slightly smaller than the button size. Remember to include the number of rows or stitches each buttonhole will use.

In single ribbing (knit 1, purl 1), the eyelet buttonhole worked in a center purl stitch is almost invisible. Begin on a right side row; work to the buttonhole placement and then work a yarn over, knit two stitches together, and finish the row in the pattern. On the next row, work the yarn over as a regular stitch. In a vertical band of knit 2, purl 2 ribbing, this same buttonhole can be worked with two purl stitches at the center of the right side rows. Work to the first center purl stitch, purl one, yarn over, knit two stitches together (1 purl stitch, 1 knit stitch); finish the row. Different yarn weights change the buttonhole size, so the

Sew the shoulders together with a horizontal seam.

Mark the neck to pick up the right number of stitches for the neck ribbing.

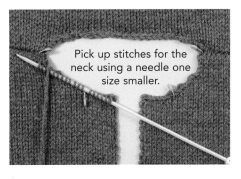
Pick up stitches for the neck using a needle one size smaller.

Pick up the stitches for the Right Front vertical buttonhole band to coordinate with the completed and marked button band on the Left Front.

eyelet works well in thick or thin yarns.

The easiest buttonhole for a horizontal band and for larger buttonholes is the two-row buttonhole; it is worked as follows: Right side row—work to the buttonhole placement, bind off the buttonhole stitches; finish the row. Next row—work to within one stitch of the buttonhole; work the front and back loops of the same stitch. Cast on one less stitch than the number bound off; finish the row.

Button Selection Tips

• To create the correct size buttonhole, buy the buttons before you make buttonholes. Also take your gauge swatch when buying buttons; it is a better visual than a skein of yarn. If you can't find a perfect color match, choose buttons that contrast.
• Glassy, glittery buttons work well with dressy yarns. Bone, wood, or metal are better for heavy outdoor garments. Buttons are made with or without a shank; shank buttons are suitable for all yarn weights and are the best choice for thick, bulky knits.
• Buy washable buttons if you plan to wash the garment and dry-cleanable ones if the garment (yarn) will require dry-cleaning. Pay attention to special-care instructions with the buttons.

SIZES: S (M, L, XL, 2X)
Shown in size M. When only one number is given, it applies to all sizes. *Note: For ease in working, circle all numbers pertaining to your size.*

FINISHED MEASUREMENTS
Underarm (buttoned) = 37 (42, 47, 52, 57)"

YARN
Lion Brand Wool-Ease Chunky (Art. 630;) 80% acrylic, 20% wool, 5 oz. (143 g); 153 yds. (140 m); chunky weight

• 5 (6, 7, 8, 9) balls #173 Willow

NEEDLES, BUTTONS, & EXTRAS
• Size 9 (5.5 mm) needles
• Size 10.5 (6.5 mm) needles OR SIZE NEEDED TO OBTAIN GAUGE
• Stitch markers
• Tapestry needle
• Seven ¾" (19 mm) buttons

GAUGE
13 sts and 18 rows = 4" (10 cm) with larger needles over Stockinette stitch. TAKE TIME TO CHECK YOUR GAUGE.

PATTERN STITCHES
2×2 RIB
Row 1 (WS): P2, *K2, P2; rep from * across.
Row 2: K2, *P2, K2; rep from * across. Rep Rows 1–2 for pat.

STOCKINETTE STITCH (St st)
Row 1 (WS): Purl.
Row 2: Knit. Rep Rows 1–2 for pat.
Note: Work all decreases and increases one stitch in from the edge.

INSTRUCTIONS
BACK
With smaller needles, cast on 62 (70, 78, 86, 94) sts. Work 2×2 Rib for 9 rows, ending with a WS row. Change to larger needles and St st. Work even until piece measures 9½ (10, 11, 11½, 12)" from beg, ending with a WS row. **Shape armholes:** Bind off 7 (8, 9, 10, 11) sts at beg of next 2 rows—48 (54, 60,

66, 72) sts. Work even until armhole measures 8½ (9, 9½, 10, 10½)", ending with a WS row. **Shape Back neck and shoulders:** Work across first 17 (19, 21, 23, 25) sts, join a new ball and bind off center 14 (16, 18, 20, 22) sts, work to end of row. Working both sides AT THE SAME TIME, bind off 2 sts at each neck edge twice. Cont in pat on rem 13 (15, 17, 19, 21) sts of each shoulder and work even until piece measures 20 (21, 22½, 23½, 24½)" from beg. Bind off all sts in pat.

RIGHT FRONT

With smaller needles, cast on 31 (35, 39, 43, 47) sts.

Foundation Row (WS): Work in 2×2 Rib across 30 (34, 38, 42, 46) sts, k1 (front edge st). Maintaining first st in Garter st (k every row) at front edge, work in 2×2 Rib for 8 more rows, ending with a WS row. Change to larger needles and St st. Keeping first st at front edge in Garter st, work in St st until piece measures same as Back to armhole, ending with a RS row. **Shape armholes:** Bind off 7 (8, 9, 10, 11) sts at beg of next row—24 (27, 30, 33, 36) sts. Work even until armhole measures 5½ (6, 6½, 6½, 7)", ending with a WS row. **Shape neck:** Bind off 6 (6, 7, 7, 7) sts at beg of next row. Cont in pat, binding off 2 sts at front edge every other row 2 (3, 3, 3, 4) times, then 1 st 1 (0, 0, 1, 0) times—13 (15, 17, 19, 21) sts. Work even until piece measures same as Back to shoulder. Bind off all sts in pat.

LEFT FRONT

With smaller needles, cast on 31 (35, 39, 43, 47) sts.

Foundation Row (WS): K1 (front edge st), work in 2×2 Rib across 30 (34, 38, 42, 46) sts. Maintaining first st in Garter st at front edge, work in 2×2 Rib for 8 more rows, ending with a WS row. Change to larger needles and St st. Keeping first st at front edge in Garter st, work to correspond to Right Front, reversing shapings.

SLEEVES (make two)

With smaller needles, cast on 26 (30, 30, 34, 34) sts. Work 2×2 Rib for 9 rows, ending with a WS row. Change to larger needles and St st. **Inc Row (RS):** K1, M1, k to last st, M1, k1. Cont in St st and rep Inc Row every 4th row 8 (5, 10, 9, 11) times more, then every 6th row 6 (9, 6, 7, 6) times—56 (60, 64, 68, 70) sts. Work even until sleeve measures 19¾ (21, 22, 22½, 23¾)" from beg. Bind off loosely in pat.

FINISHING

Block pieces to measurements. Sew Fronts to Back at shoulders.

Neckband: With RS facing and using smaller needles and starting at right neck, pick up and k the 6 (6, 7, 7, 7) bound-off sts, 12 (12, 12, 13, 14) sts along Right Front neck, 26 (30, 32, 34, 36) sts from Back neck, 12 (12, 12, 13, 14) sts along Left Front neck, and 6 (6, 7, 7, 7) bound-off sts from left neck—62 (66, 70, 74, 78) sts. Work in 2×2 Rib for 1". Bind off all sts in pat.

Left Front (Button) Band: With RS facing and using smaller needles, pick up and k62 (66, 70, 74, 78) sts evenly spaced along Left Front. Work in 2×2 Rib for 1". Bind off all sts in pat. Mark positions of 7 buttons evenly spaced on Left Front band, placing the first and last ¼" from neck and bottom edges.

Right Front (Buttonhole) Band: Work Right Front band to correspond to Left Front band, working yo, k2tog [buttonholes] opposite markers on 3rd row of rib. Work even until rib measures 1". Bind off all sts in pat.

Sew Sleeves to body. Sew body and sleeve seams. Sew on buttons. Weave in all ends. Block lightly, if needed.

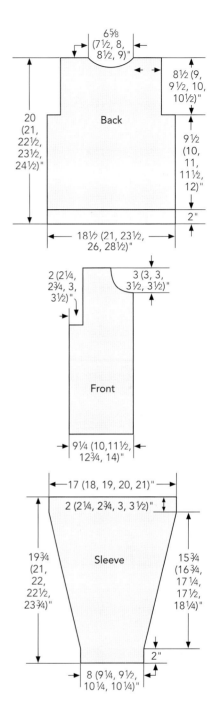

sleeveless knitted TURTLENECK

Suitable for a first project, this versatile top has subtle color variation and beautiful texture.

DESIGN: LIDIA KARABINECH

SKILL LEVEL: EASY

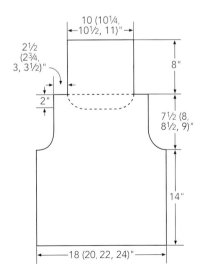

SIZES: S (M, L, XL)
Shown in Size S. When only one number is given, it applies to all sizes. *Note: For ease in working, before you begin the pattern, circle all numbers pertaining to your size.*

FINISHED MEASUREMENTS
Bust = 36 (40, 44, 48)"
Length = 21½ (22, 22½, 23)"

YARN
Lion Brand Homespun (Art. 790); 98% acrylic, 2% polyester; 185 yds. (169 m); bulky weight

- 2, (2, 3, 3) skeins # 350 Elizabethan

NEEDLES & EXTRAS
- Size 10 (6 mm) knitting needles OR SIZE NEEDED TO OBTAIN GAUGE
- 16-inch-length circular needle in same size as that used to obtain gauge
- Stitch holders
- Stitch marker
- Tapestry needle

GAUGE
In Stockinette stitch (ST st), 13 sts and 19 rows = 4"/10 cm.

Note: 1 st each edge is used as a selvage. These sts are not reflected in the finished measurements.

INSTRUCTIONS
BACK
Beginning at the lower edge, cast on 60 (67, 74, 80) sts.
Row 1 (RS): (K1, p1) across.
Row 2: (P1, k1) across.
Rep Rows 1–2 four times more.
Change to St st (k RS rows, p WS rows). Work even to 14" from beg, end with WS row.

Shape armholes: Bind off 2 (3, 4, 4) sts at beg of next 2 rows. Dec Row (RS): Sl1 kwise, k1, p1, k2tog, knit to last 5 sts, ssk, k1, p1, k1. WS Rows: Sl1 pwise, p1, k1, purl to last 3 sts, k1, p2. Rep Dec Row 3 (4, 5, 6) times more—48 (51, 54, 58) sts.

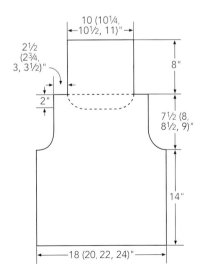 diagram labels:

10 (10¼, 10½, 11)"

2½ (2¾, 3, 3½)"

8"

2"

7½ (8, 8½, 9)"

14"

18 (20, 22, 24)"

Make armhole edging: **Row 1 (RS):** Sl1 kwise, k1, p1, k to last 3 sts, p1, k2. **Row 2:** Sl1 pwise, p1, k1, purl to last 3 sts, k1, p2. Rep Rows 1–2 to 21½ (22, 22½, 23)" from beg, ending with a WS row.

Shape shoulders and neck: Bind off 8 (9, 10, 11) sts at beg of next 2 rows. Place rem 32 (33, 34, 36) sts onto stitch holder for back of neck.

FRONT

Work as for Back to 19½ (20, 20½, 21)" from beg, ending with a WS row.

Shape neck: **Dec Row (RS):** Sl1 kwise, k1, p1, k 7 (8, 9, 10), ssk, k1, place next 22 (23, 24, 26) sts onto holder. Attach a separate strand of yarn to other side and work rem sts as follows: K1, k2tog, k7 (8, 9, 10), p1, k2. Working shoulders separately and AT THE SAME TIME, rep Dec Row every other row four times more. When Front measures same as Back, bind off 8 (9, 10, 11) sts for each shoulder.

FINISHING

Join shoulders and side seams. Make turtleneck: With RS facing and circular needle, k32 (33, 34, 36) sts from back holder, pick up and k6 sts along neck edge, k22 (23, 24, 26) sts from front holder, pick up and k 6 sts—66 (68, 70, 74) sts. Pm to indicate beg of rnd. Join. **Rnd 1:** (K1, p1) around. Rep Rnd 1 until turtleneck measures 8". Bind off loosely.

cable
twin set

Soft white yarn clearly shows off the texture of cables on this pretty sweater set.

DESIGN: LIDIA KARABINECH

SKILL LEVEL: INTERMEDIATE

SIZES: S (M, L, XL)

Shown in Size M. When only one number is given, it applies to all sizes.

Note: For ease in working, circle all numbers pertaining to your size.

FINISHED MEASUREMENTS

Underarm/Shell = 34 (36, 40, 42)"
Underarm/Cardigan (buttoned) = 38 (40, 44, 46)"

YARN

Lion Brand Wool-Ease (Art. 620);
80% acrylic, 20% wool; 2.5 oz. (71 g);
162 yds. (148 m); worsted weight

- Shell: 3 (3, 4, 4) balls #99 Fisherman
- Cardigan: 8 (8, 9, 9) balls #99 Fisherman

NEEDLES, BUTTONS, & EXTRAS

- Size 7 (4.5 mm) needles OR SIZE NEEDED TO OBTAIN GAUGE
- Size 8 (5 mm) needles OR SIZE NEEDED TO OBTAIN GAUGE
- Cable needle (cn)
- Stitch holders
- Stitch markers
- Six ⅝" (15 mm) buttons

GAUGE

18 sts and 24 rows = 4" (10 cm) over Seed Stitch using larger needles.
TAKE TIME TO CHECK YOUR GAUGE.

Note: Work all increases and decreases one stitch in from edge.

SPECIAL ABBREVIATIONS

2/2 RC = Sl 2 sts to cn and hold in back of work, k2, then k2 from cn
2/2 LC = Sl 2 sts to cn and hold in front of work, k2, then k2 from cn
2/1 RPC = Sl 1 st to cn and hold in back of work, k2, then p1 from cn
2/1 LPC = Sl 2 sts to cn and hold in front of work, p1, then k2 from cn
2/2 RPC = Sl 2 sts to cn and hold in back of work, k2, then p2 from cn
2/2 LPC = Sl 2 sts to cn and hold in front of work, p2, then k2 from cn

PATTERN STITCHES

SEED STITCH

Row 1: *K1, p1*, rep to end.
Row 2: Knit the purl sts, purl the knit sts.
Rep Row 2 for pat.

SLIP RIB

Row 1: K1, p1.
Rows 2 and 4 (WS): K the knit and p the purl sts.
Row 3: Sl 1 with yarn in back, p1.
Rep Rows 3–4 for pat.

CABLE A (20 sts)

Row 1: P4, 2/2 RC, p4, 2/2 LC, p4.
Row 2 and all WS Rows: K the knit and p the purl sts.
Row 3: P3, 2/1 RPC, 2/1 LPC, p2, 2/1 RPC, 2/1 LPC, p3.
Row 5: P2, 2/1 RPC, p2, 2/1 LPC, 2/1 RPC, p2, 2/1 LPC, p2.

Rows 7 and 11: P2, k2, p4, 2/2 RC, p4, k2, p2.

Row 9: P2, k2, p4, k4, p4, k2, p2.

Row 13: P2, 2/1 LPC, p2, 2/1 RPC, 2/1 LPC, p2, 2/1 RPC, p2.

Row 15: P3, 2/1 LPC, 2/1 RPC, p2, 2/1 LPC, 2/1 RPC, p3.

Row 17: Rep Row 1.

Row 19: P4, k4, p4, k4, p4.

Row 20: K the knit and p the purl sts.

Rep Rows 1–20 for pat.

Cable B (12 sts)

Row 1: P1, k4, 2/2 RPC, p1.

Row 2 and All WS Rows: K the knit and p the purl sts.

Row 3: P1, 2/2 RPC, 2/2 RC, p3.

Row 5: P1, k2, 2/2 RPC, 2/2 LPC, p1.

Row 7: P1, 2/2 RC, p4, k2, p1.

Row 8: K the knit and p the purl sts.

Rep Rows 1–8 for pat.

Cable C (12 sts)

Row 1: P1, 2/2 LPC, p2, k4, p1.

Row 2 and all WS rows: K the knit and p the purl sts.

Row 3: P3, 2/2 LC, 2/2 LPC, p1.

Row 5: P1, 2/2 RPC, 2/2 LPC, k2, p1.

Row 7: P1, k2, p4, 2/2 LC, p1.

Row 8: K the knit and p the purl sts.

Repeat Rows 1–8 for pat.

INSTRUCTIONS FOR SHELL
BACK

With smaller needles, cast on 77 (82, 87, 92) sts. Work in k1, p1 Rib for 8 rows. Change to larger needles and work Seed st for 4 rows. Dec Row: K1, k2tog, work to last 3 sts, ssk, k1. Rep Dec Row every 12 rows 2 times more—71 (76, 81, 86) sts. Work even for 10 rows. Inc Row: K1, M1, work to last st, M1, k1. Rep Inc Row every 10 rows 2 times more—77 (82, 87, 92) sts. Shape armholes: Bind off 3 (3, 3, 4) sts at beg of next 2 rows, then 2 sts at beg of next 2 rows. Dec Row: Work 4 sts Slip Rib (beg with k1), ssk, work in Seed st to last 6 sts, k2tog, work 4 sts Slip Rib (beg with p1). Rep Dec Row every other row 4 (5, 6, 6) times more—57 (60, 63, 66) sts. Work even until armhole measures 7½ (8, 8¼, 9)", ending with a WS row.

Shape shoulders and neck: Bind off 7 sts at beg of next 4 (2, 0, 0) rows, then 8 sts at beg of next 0 (2, 4, 2) rows, then 9 sts at beg of next 0 (0, 0, 2) rows. AT SAME TIME, place center 25 (26, 27, 28) sts on a holder for neck, join second ball of yarn and working both sides at once, bind off 2 sts from each neck edge once.

FRONT

With smaller needles, cast on 80 (84, 88, 92) sts. Work in k1, p1 Rib for 8 rows. Change to larger needles. Setup Row (RS): Work first 28 (30, 32, 34) sts in Seed st, pm, work 4 sts Slip Rib (beg with p1), pm, work Cable A over next 16 sts inc 4 sts evenly spaced across cable, pm, work 4 sts Slip Rib (beg with k1), pm, work 28 (30, 32, 34) sts in Seed st—84 (88, 92, 96) sts. Work 3 rows even, maintaining pats. Dec Row: K1, k2tog, work in pat to last 3 sts, ssk, k1. Rep Dec Row every 12 rows 2 times more—78 (82, 86, 90) sts. Work even for 10 rows.

Inc Row: K1, M1, work in pat to last st, M1, k1. Rep Inc Row every 10 rows 2 more times—84 (88, 92, 96) sts. Shape armholes: Bind off 3 (3, 3, 4) sts at beg of next 2 rows, then 2 sts at beg of next 2 rows. Dec Row: Work 4 sts Slip Rib (beg with k1), k2tog, work in pat to last 6 sts, ssk, work 4 sts Slip Rib (beg with p1). Rep Dec Row every other row 5 (6, 6, 6) more times—62 (64, 68, 70) sts. Work even until armhole measures 5¼ (5¾, 6¼, 6¾)", ending with a WS row. Shape neck and shoulders–Dec Row: Work 19 (20, 22, 23) sts in pat, k2tog, p1, place next 18 sts on a holder, join second ball of yarn, p1, ssk, work in pat to end. Working both sides at once, rep Dec Row every other row 10 (10, 12, 12) times more. AT THE SAME TIME, when armhole measures as for Back, shape shoulders as for Back.

FINISHING

Sew shoulder and side seams. Shape neckband: With RS facing, k across 25 (26, 27, 28) sts from back neck holder, pick up and k15 (15, 16, 16) sts along neck edge, k across 18 sts from front neck holder, pick up and k14 (15, 15, 16) sts—72 (74, 76, 78) sts. Join rnd. Work in k1, p1 Rib for 3 rnds. Bind off.

INSTRUCTIONS FOR CARDIGAN
BACK

Cast on 92 (96, 104, 108) sts. Work in k1, p1 rib for 6 rows. Setup Row (RS): Work first 10 (12, 16, 16) sts in Seed st, pm, work 6 sts Slip Rib (beg with p1), pm, work Cable A over next 16 sts inc 4 sts evenly spaced across cable, pm, * work 6 (6, 6, 8) sts Slip Rib, pm, work Cable A over next 16 sts inc 4 sts evenly spaced across cable, pm, rep from * once more; work 6 sts Slip Rib (beg with k1), pm, work 10 (12, 16, 16) sts in Seed st—104 (108, 116, 120) sts. Work even in pat until piece measures 14" from beg, ending with a WS row. Shape armholes: Bind off 3 (3, 3, 4) sts at beg of next 2 rows, then 2 sts at beg of next 2 rows. Dec Row: K1, ssk, work in pat to last 3 sts, k2tog, k1. Rep Dec Row every other row 3 (4, 5, 5) times more—86 (88, 94, 96) sts. Work even until armhole measures 8 (8½, 9, 9½)", ending with a WS row. Shape shoulders and back neck: Bind off 8 sts at beg of 4 (6, 2, 0) rows, then 9 sts at beg of 0 (0, 4, 6) rows, then 7 sts at beg of 2 (0, 0, 0) rows. Place rem 40 (40, 42, 42) sts on a stitch holder for back neck.

LEFT FRONT

Cast on 56 (58, 62, 66) sts. Work in k1, p1 rib for 6 rows. Setup Row (RS): Work 10 (12, 16, 16) sts in Seed st, pm, work 6 sts Slip Rib (beg with p1), pm, work Cable A over next 16 sts inc 4 sts evenly spaced across cable, pm, work 6 (6, 6, 8) sts Slip Rib (beg with k1), pm, work Cable C over next 10 sts increasing 2 sts evenly spaced across cable, pm, work 8 sts Slip Rib (for front band)—62 (64, 68, 70) sts. Work even in pat until piece measures 14" from beg, ending with a WS row. Shape armhole (RS): Bind off 3 (3, 3, 4) sts at beg of next row, then 2 sts at beg of next RS row. Next RS Row: K1, ssk, work in pat to end. Rep Dec Row 3 (5, 6, 6) times more every other row—53 (53, 56, 57) sts. Work even until armhole measures 5½ (6, 6½, 7)", ending with a RS row. Shape Front neck and shoulder (WS): Place 12 sts on a holder for neckband, work to end. Next WS Row: Bind off 2 sts at beg of row 9 (8, 9, 9) times, then 1 st at beg of row 0 (1, 0, 0) times. AT THE SAME TIME, when armhole measures same as Back and beg at shoulder edge, bind off 7 sts 3 (3, 3, 3) times at shoulder; then bind off rem sts.

RIGHT FRONT

Work as for Left Front, reversing pats and shaping. Work Cable B instead of Cable C. On Left Front, mark positions for 6 buttons evenly spaced between ½" from bottom edge and middle of neckband. Work buttonholes in center of 8-st band opposite marked button positions as follows: (RS) Rib 4, yo, k2tog, Rib 2, work pats to end.

SLEEVES (make two)

Cast on 38 (42, 46, 50) sts. Work in k1, p1 Rib for 6 rows. **Setup Row (RS):** Work 7 (9, 11, 13) sts in Seed st, pm, work 4 sts Slip Rib (beg p1); pm, work Cable A over next 16 sts inc 4 sts evenly spaced across cable, pm, work 4 sts Slip Rib (beg k1), pm, work 7 (9, 11, 13) sts in Seed st—42 (46, 50, 54) sts. Work even until piece measures 4" from beg, ending with a WS row. **Inc Row:** K1, M1, work in pat to last st, M1, k1. Rep Inc Row every 8 rows 10 times more, working new sts in Seed—64 (68, 72, 76) sts. Work even until piece measures 18" from beg, ending with a WS row. **Shape cap:** Bind off 3 sts at beg of next 2 rows, then 2 sts at beg of next 2 rows. **Dec Row:** K2, ssk, work in pats to last 4 sts, k2tog, k2. Rep Dec Row every other row 15, (16, 17, 18) times more. Bind off rem 22 (24, 26, 28) sts.

FINISHING

Sew shoulders together. **Shape neckband:** With RS facing and using smaller needles, work k1, p1 Rib across 12 sts from front holder, pick up and k12 (13, 14, 15) sts along front edge, Rib across 40 (40, 42, 42) sts from back holder, pick up and k12 (13, 14, 15) sts, rib 12 sts from front holder—88 (90, 94, 96) sts. Work in k1, p1 rib for 6 rows. Bind off loosely in rib.

Block pieces. Sew sleeves into armholes. Sew side and sleeve seams. Sew on buttons. Weave in loose ends.

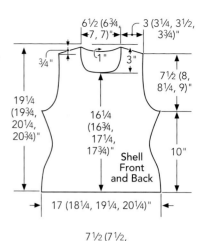

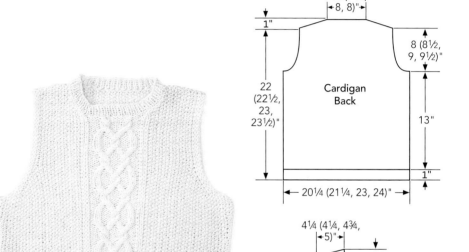

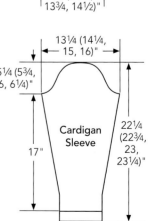

two-tone
PLAITED PULLOVER

SIZES: S (M, L, XL, 2X)
Shown in Size L. When only one number is given, it applies to all sizes. *Note: For ease in working, circle all numbers pertaining to your size.*

FINISHED MEASUREMENTS
Underarm = 41 (46, 51, 56, 61)"

YARNS
Lion Brand Chunky USA (Art. 420); 100% acrylic; 4 oz. (113 g); 155 yds. (142 m); chunky weight

- 5 (6, 6, 7, 8) balls #099 Fisherman (MC)
- 2 (3, 3, 3, 4) balls #152 Skyscraper Grey (CC)

NEEDLES & EXTRAS
- Size 9 (5.5 mm) needles
- Size 9 (5.5 mm) 16" circular needle
- Size 10.5 (6.5 mm) needles OR SIZE NEEDED TO OBTAIN GAUGE
- Cable needle (cn)
- Stitch markers
- Tapestry needle

GAUGE
12 sts and 23 rows = 4" (10 cm) over Box Stitch pat using larger needles.
27 sts Plait Cable Panel = 5½" using larger needles.
TAKE TIME TO CHECK YOUR GAUGE.

SPECIAL ABBREVIATIONS
3/3 RC = Slip 3 sts to cn and hold in back of work; K3; K3 from cn
3/3 LC = Slip 3 sts to cn and hold in front of work; K3; K3 from cn

PATTERN STITCHES
BOX STITCH
Row 1 (RS): K2, *p2, k2; rep from * across.
Rows 2 and 3: P2; *k2, p2; rep from * across.
Row 4: Rep Row 1. Rep these 4 rows for pat.

PLAIT CABLE (panel of 27 sts)
Row 1 (RS): *K3, 3/3 RC; rep from * twice.
Rows 2, 4, 6 and 8: Purl.
Rows 3 and 7: Knit.
Row 5: *3/3 LC, k3; rep from * twice. Rep Rows 1–8 for pat.

INSTRUCTIONS
BACK
With smaller needles and CC, cast on 71 (79, 87, 95,103) sts.
Row 1 (WS): K2; [p2, k2] 5 (6, 7, 8, 9) times; pm; [p3, k3] 4 times; p3; pm; [k2, p2] 5 (6, 7, 8, 9) times; k2.
Row 2: P2; [k2, p2] 5 (6, 7, 8, 9) times; sl marker; k3; [p3, k3] 4 times; pm; [p2, k2] 5 (6, 7, 8, 9) times; p2. Rep these 2 rows 2 3 (3, 3, 4, 4) times more, ending with a RS row. Change to larger needles, cut yarn, and remove markers.
Foundation Row (WS): With MC, p22 (26, 30, 34, 38) sts; join CC, p27; join second ball CC, p22 (26, 30, 34, 38).

Next row: Maintain colors as set and work Row 1 of pat sts as follows: 22 (26, 30, 34, 38) sts in Box Stitch, 27 sts of Plait Cable Panel, 22 (26, 30, 34, 38) sts in Box Stitch. Cont even in pats until piece measures 15 (15½, 15¾, 16½, 16¾)" from beg, ending with a WS row.

Shape armholes: Bind off 6 (7, 8, 9, 10) sts at beg next 2 rows—59 (65, 71, 77, 83) sts. Cont even in pat until piece measures 8¾ (9, 9¼, 9¾ ,10)" above armholes. End with a WS row. Shape back neck and shoulders: Maintain colors and work 17 (20, 22, 24, 27) sts in pat, bind off center 25 (25, 27, 29, 29) sts, work rem 17 (20, 22, 24, 27) sts in pat. Working both sides at the same time, bind off 5 (6, 6, 7, 8) sts at shoulder edge twice, then 4 (5, 7, 7, 8) sts once, and AT THE SAME TIME, bind off 1 st at each neck edge 3 times—no sts rem.

FRONT
Work same as for Back until piece measures 22 (22¾, 23, 24¼, 24¾)" from beg. Maintain colors and work across 21 (24, 27, 30, 33) sts in pat, bind off center 17 sts, work rem 21 (24, 27, 30, 33) sts in pat. Working both sides AT THE SAME TIME, bind off at each neck edge 2 sts 2 (2, 2, 3, 3) times, then one st 3 (3, 4, 3, 3) times—14 (17, 19, 21, 24) sts rem. Work even until piece measures same as Back to shoulders. Shape shoulders same as for Back—no sts rem.

Once you've knitted a cable or two, you'll be eager to complete this pretty two-tone pullover that will show off your talent and good taste.

DESIGN: KATHY ZIMMERMAN

SKILL LEVEL: INTERMEDIATE

SLEEVES (make two)

With smaller needles and CC, cast on 26 (26, 30, 30, 30) sts.

Row 1 (WS): K2, [p2, k2] 6 (6, 7, 7, 7) times.

Row 2: P2, [k2, p2] 6 (6, 7, 7, 7) times. Rep these 2 rows 4 times more, ending with a RS row. Cut CC; join MC and change to larger needles. P 1 row.

Next Row: Work Row 1 of Box Stitch. Cont in pat and AT THE SAME TIME, inc 1 st at each end every 4th row 2 (4, 2, 3, 4) times, every 6th row 3 (6, 5, 6, 7) times, every 8th row 8 (5, 7, 6, 5) times, working new sts into pat—52 (56, 58, 60, 62) sts. Work even until piece measures 19¾ (20¼, 21, 21¾, 22¼)". Bind off all sts.

FINISHING

Sew Front to Back at shoulders.

Make neckband: With RS facing, using circular needle and CC, and beginning at left shoulder seam, pick up and k11 (11, 14, 14, 14) sts of Front at left neck, 17 sts at Front neck center, 11 (11, 14, 14, 14) sts of Front at right neck, and 33 (33, 35, 39, 39) sts along Back neck—72 (72, 80, 84, 84) sts. Work k2, p2 ribbing for 1". Bind off all sts loosely in pat. Attach sleeves to body. Sew side and sleeve seams.

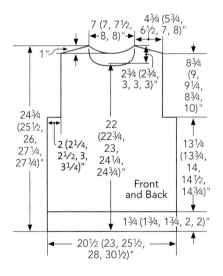

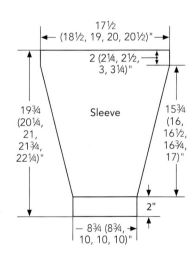

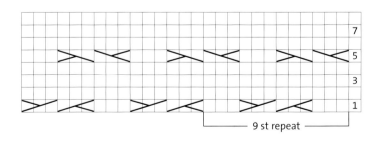

cowl neck
SWEATER

Large-gauge
yarn, ease of
knitting, and
stylish good
looks ensure
that even
newcomers to
knitting will
quickly finish
this pretty
casual-wear
sweater.

DESIGN: LIDIA KARABINECH

SKILL LEVEL: EASY

SIZES: S (M, L, XL)

Shown in size S.

The pattern is written for the smallest size with changes for larger sizes indicated in parentheses. When only one number is given, it applies to all sizes. *Note: For ease in working, before you begin the pattern, circle all numbers pertaining to your size.*

FINISHED MEASUREMENTS

Bust = 36 (40, 44, 48)"
Length = 22½ (23, 23½, 24)"

YARN

Lion Brand Homespun (Art. 790);
98% acrylic, 2% polyester; 185 yds. (169 m);
bulky weight

- 4 (4, 5, 5) balls Romanesque #343

NEEDLES & EXTRAS

- Size 10 (6 mm) straight knitting needles OR SIZE NEEDED TO OBTAIN GAUGE
- Size 9 (5.5 mm), size 10½ (6.5 mm), and size 11 (8 mm) 16" circular needles
- Stitch holder
- Ring-type stitch markers
- Tapestry needle

GAUGE

In Stockinette Stitch (St st) with straight needles, 13 sts and 19 rows = 4"(10 cm) over St st (knit 1 row, purl 1 row).
TAKE TIME TO CHECK YOUR GAUGE.

SPECIAL ABBREVIATIONS

Ssk: Sl next 2 sts singly to right needle knitwise, insert tip of left needle through front lp of both sts and k tog.

M1: Lift the horizontal thread lying between needles and place onto left needle; k in back lp of this new st.

Note: 1 st at each edge is a selvage st and is not reflected in the finished measurements.

INSTRUCTIONS
BACK

Beginning at the lower edge, cast on 60 (67, 74, 80) sts. K 6 rows for Garter st band. Beg with a k row, work St st (k RS rows, p WS rows) for 10 rows.

Dec Row (RS): K1, ssk, k across to last 3 sts, k2tog, k1. Rep Dec Row every 10th row, twice more * 54 (61, 68, 74) sts. Work 9 rows even.

Inc Row (RS): K1, M1, k across to last st, M1, k1. Rep Inc Row every 10th row, twice more * 60 (67, 74, 80) sts. Work even to 15" from beg, ending with a WS row. **Shape armholes:** Bind off 2 (3, 4, 4) sts at beg of next 2 rows. **Dec Row (RS):** K2, k2tog, k across to last 4 sts, ssk, k2. Rep Dec Row every other row 10 (12, 13, 15) times more—34 (35, 38, 40) sts. Continue in pat to 22½ (23, 23½, 24)" from beg, ending with a WS row. **Shape shoulders and neck:**

Bind off 6 (6, 7, 7) sts at the beg of the next 2 rows. Bind off rem 22 (23, 24, 26) sts for back neck.

FRONT

Work as for Back to 18 (18, 18½, 19)" from beg, ending with a WS row. Place markers (pm) on either side of center 10 (11, 12, 14) sts. **Shape neck:** Cont armhole shaping and work to first marker, place 10 (11, 12, 14) sts onto holder; join a 2nd skein of yarn and work to end of row. Working shoulders separately and AT THE SAME TIME, dec 1 st each neck edge every other row 6 times. Cont in pat on rem 6 (6, 7, 7) sts for each shoulder same length as Back. Shape shoulders as for Back.

SLEEVES (make two)

Beg at lower edge, cast on 33 (36, 39, 43) sts. K 4 rows for Garter st band. Beg with a k row, work 8 rows St st.

Dec Row (RS): K1, k2tog, k across to last 3 sts, ssk, k1. Rep Dec Row every 6th row twice more—27 (30, 33, 37) sts. Work 7 rows St st.

Inc Row (RS): K1, M1, k across to last st, M1, k1. Rep Inc Row every 8th row 7 times more—43 (46, 49, 53) sts. Work even to 19" from beg, ending with a WS row. **Shape sleeve caps:** Bind off 2 (3, 4, 4) sts at beg of next 2 rows. **Dec Row (RS):** K2, k2tog, k across to last 4 sts, ssk, k2. Rep Dec Row every other row 12 (13, 14, 16) times more. Bind off rem 13 (12, 11, 11) sts.

FINISHING

Block pieces to measurements. Join shoulder seams. Set in sleeves. Join underarm and side seams.

COWL NECK

With WS facing and size 9 circular needle, pick up and k22 (23, 24, 26) sts evenly spaced along back neck. Pick up and k16 (17, 18, 19) sts evenly along side of neck; work across 10 (11, 12, 14) sts from holder. Pick up and k16 (17, 18, 19) sts evenly along side of neck. Pm to indicate beg of rnd; join. K 5 rnds for St st. Change to size 10½ needle; k 20 rnds. Change to size 11 needle; cont k every rnd until collar measures 9". P 1 rnd, k 1 rnd, p 1 rnd for Garter st band. Bind off loosely and knitwise.

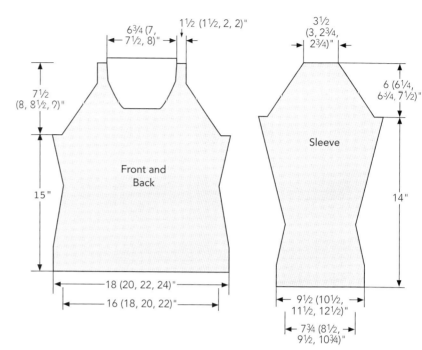

shawl collar
JACKET

This flirty knitted jacket, with a shawl collar and uneven hem, is a flattering style for many figures.

DESIGN: LILY CHIN

SKILL LEVEL: EASY

SIZES: S (M, L, XL, XXL)
Shown in Size S; additional sizes are shown in parentheses. When only one number is given, it applies to all sizes. *Note: For ease in working, before you begin the pattern, circle all numbers pertaining to your size.*

FINISHED MEASUREMENTS
Underarm= 40 (44, 48, 52, 56)"
Length = 24 (24½, 25, 25½, 26)"

YARN
Lion Brand Homespun (Art. 790); 98% acrylic, 2% polyester; 185 yds. (169 m); bulky weight

● 5 (5, 6, 7, 8) skeins #339 Creole

NEEDLES, BUTTONS & EXTRAS
● Size 10 (6 mm) knitting needles OR SIZE NEEDED TO OBTAIN GAUGE
● 29" circular needle of same size as that used to obtain gauge
● Yarn needle.

GAUGE
12 sts and 22 rows = 4" (10cm) in Garter st (k every row). TAKE TIME TO CHECK YOUR GAUGE.

Note: Front and Back are different lengths.

INSTRUCTIONS
BACK
Cast on 62 (68, 74, 80, 86) sts.

Body Pattern (Garter Stitch): ALL ROWS— Sl first st as if to k, k across. Cont in pat until piece measures approx 14½" from beg.

Shape armholes: Continue in Garter st, bind off 2 sts at beg of next 2 rows * 58 (64, 70, 76, 82) sts. Keep first and last sts in St st (k on RS, p on WS) and dec 1 st from each end after first and before last sts on next row and every other row for 3 (5, 6, 7, 9) times more. Work even on 50 (52, 56, 60, 62) sts until piece measures 22½ (23, 23½, 24, 24½)" from beg, ending with a WS row. **Shape shoulders and neck:** Cont in Garter st and bind off first 3 sts; mark center 10 (12, 14, 14, 16) sts. **Next Row (RS):** Bind off first 3 sts, then bind off center 10 (12, 14, 14, 16) sts, complete row—34 (34, 36, 40, 40) sts. Join ball of yarn to other shoulder. Working shoulders AT THE SAME TIME and with separate strands, bind off 3 sts from each shoulder edge 2 (2, 1, 0, 0) time(s), then bind off 4 sts from each shoulder edge 1 (1, 2, 3, 3) time(s). AT THE SAME TIME, bind off 2 (2, 2, 3, 3) sts from each neck edge over next 2 rows, then dec 1 st from each neck edge on next RS row. Bind off rem 4 sts for each shoulder.

RIGHT FRONT

Cast on 23 (25, 27, 29, 31) sts. Work in Garter st as for Back until piece measures approximately 11½" from beg, ending with a RS row. **Shape armholes:** Continue in Garter st, bind off 2 sts at beg of next row. Keeping armhole edge st in St st, dec 1 st from armhole edge before last st on next row and every other row 3 (5, 6, 7, 9) times more. Work even on 17 (17, 18, 19, 19) sts until piece measures approximately 19½ (20, 20½, 21, 21½)" from beg, ending with a RS row. **Shape shoulders:** Bind off 3 sts from shoulder edge on next row and every other row 2 (2, 1, 0, 0) times more, then bind off 4 sts from shoulder edge every other row 2 (2, 3, 4, 4) times.

LEFT FRONT

Work as for Right Front, reversing all shaping.

SLEEVES (make two)

Cast on 32 (33, 34, 35, 36) sts. Work in Garter st as for Back for 4". Inc 1 st at each end on next row, then every 6th row 0 (0, 1, 6, 12) time(s), every 8th row 0 (5, 9, 5, 0) times, and every 10th row 8 (4, 0, 0, 0) times. Work even in pat on 50 (53, 56, 59, 62) sts until piece measures approximately 21 (20½, 20, 19½, 19)" total from beg, ending with a WS row. **Shape sleeve caps:** Cont in Garter st and bind off 2 sts at beg of next 2 rows. Keep first and last sts in St st and dec 1 st from each end after first and before last sts on next row and every other row 3 (5, 6, 8, 9) times more. Bind off rem 38 (37, 38, 37, 38) sts on next RS row.

FINISHING

Block pieces to measurements. Sew shoulder seams. Set in sleeves, reversing front/back of seam at bottom 2". Sew sleeve seams. Sew side seams leaving bottom 4½" of Front and 7½" of Back free.

SHAWL COLLAR

With RS facing and circular needle, beg at bottom of Right Front edge. Skip first 3", pick up and k 55 (56, 57, 59, 60) sts evenly across the rem 18 (18½, 19, 19½, 20)" to shoulder of Front edge. Pick up and k20 (22, 24, 26, 28) sts evenly across back neck, pick up and k55 (56, 57, 59, 60) sts evenly across top 18 (18½, 19, 19½, 20)" of Left Front edge leaving rem 3" of lower edge free—130 (134, 138, 144, 148) sts. **Work Garter st as follows:** ALL ROWS—Sl first st as if to k, k across. Work until collar measures 6 (6½, 7, 7½, 8)" from beg. Bind off loosely.

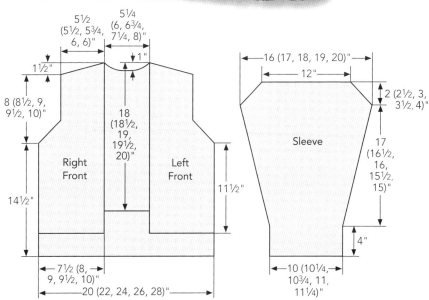

quick cable
SWEATER

With large needles, neutral-color chunky yarn, and a weekend to spare, you can quickly knit this cropped length pullover with a mock turtleneck and cable front .

DESIGN: TRACI BUNKERS

SKILL LEVEL: INTERMEDIATE

SIZES: S (M, L, XL)

Shown in Size M. When only one number is given, it applies to all sizes. *Note: For ease in working, circle all numbers pertaining to your size.*

FINISHED MEASUREMENTS

Underarm = 38 (44, 50, 56)"

YARN

Lion Brand Wool-Ease Thick & Quick (Art. 640); 86% acrylic, 10% wool, 4% rayon; 6 oz. (171 g); 108 yds. (99 m); super bulky weight

- 6 (6, 8, 9) balls #402 Wheat

NEEDLES & EXTRAS

- Size 11 (8 mm) needles OR SIZE NEEDED TO OBTAIN GAUGE
- Size 11 (8 mm) 16" circular needle
- Cable needle (cn)
- Stitch markers
- Stitch holders
- Tapestry needle

GAUGE

10 sts and 14 rows = 4" over Rib pat using size 11 (8 mm) needles.
12-stitch Cable Panel is approx 4" wide.
TAKE TIME TO CHECK YOUR GAUGE.

SPECIAL ABBREVIATIONS

4/4 LC = Slip next 4 stitches to cable needle and hold in front of work, k4, k4 from cable needle
4/4 RC = Slip next 4 stitches to cable needle and hold in back of work, k4, k4 from cable needle

PATTERN STITCHES

RIB PATTERN

RS Rows: P2, *k5, p2; rep from* across.
WS Rows: K2, *p5, k2; rep from* across.

CABLE PATTERN (over 12 stitches)

Row 1 (WS): P12.
Row 2: K12.
Row 3: P12.
Row 4: 4/4 LC, k4.
Rows 5–11: Rep Rows 1 and 2 three times, then Row 1 once more.
Row 12: K4, 4/4 RC.
Rows 13–16: Rep Rows 1 and 2 twice.
Rep Rows 1–16 for Cable Panel pat.

Notes: See page 43 for 3-needle bind-off. Work all increases and decreases one stitch in from edge of work.

INSTRUCTIONS
BACK

Cast on 46 (54, 60, 68) sts. Set up pat as follows:
Setup Row 1 (RS): K3 (0, 3, 0), p2, [k5, p2] 2 (3, 3, 4) times, place marker (pm), k8, pm, [p2, k5] 2 (3, 3, 4) times, p2, k3 (0, 3, 0).
Setup Row 2: P3 (0, 3, 0), k2, [p5, k2] 2 (3, 3, 4) times, p8, [k2, p5] 2 (3, 3, 4) times, k2, p3 (0, 3, 0).
Setup Row 3: K3 (0, 3, 0), p2, [k5, p2] 2 (3, 3, 4) times, [k into front and back of next st, k1] 4 times, [p2, k5] 2 (3, 3, 4) times, p2, k3 (0, 3, 0) 50 (58, 64, 72) sts and 12 sts between markers for Cable Panel.
Begin Cable Panel (WS): Work in est Rib pat to marker, work Row 1 of Cable Panel between markers, work in Rib pat to end. Work even in pat as est until piece measures 12½ (13½, 14, 15)" from beg, ending with a WS row.

Shape armholes: Bind off 3 (7, 7, 7) sts at beg of next 2 rows—44 (44, 50, 58) sts. Work even until armhole measures 8 (8½, 9, 9½)", ending with a RS row. **Next Row (WS):** Work in pat to marker, [p1, p2tog] 4 times, work in pat to end. **Next Row:** Work 12 (12, 14, 18) sts for shoulder and place onto holder, bind off next 16 (16, 18, 18) sts for Back neck, work rem 12 (12, 14, 18) sts for shoulder and place onto holder.

FRONT

Work as for Back until armhole measures 5 (5½, 5½, 6)", ending with a RS row. **Next Row:** Work in pat to marker, [p1, p2tog] 4 times, work in pat to end. Shape Front neck. **Next Row:** Work in pat to marker, join second ball of yarn and bind off center 8 sts for Front neck, work in pat to end. Working both sides at the same time, at each neck edge bind off 2 sts once, then dec 1 st every other row 2 (2, 3, 3) times—12 (12, 14, 18) sts rem each shoulder. Work even until armhole measures same as Back. Place shoulder sts onto holder.

SLEEVES (make two)

Cast on 23 (23, 27, 27) sts.
Row 1 (RS): K0 (0, 2, 2), p2, [k5, p2] 3 times, k0 (0, 2, 2).
Row 2: P0 (0, 2, 2), k2, [p5, k2] 3 times, p0 (0, 2, 2).
Rep Rows 1–2 for pat and AT SAME TIME, inc 1 st each end on 5th row, then every 6 rows 8 (9, 8, 9) times more, working new sts into Rib pat—41 (43, 45, 47) sts. Work even until piece measures 18½ (20, 21, 21)" from beg. Bind off all sts. Place marker 1½ (3, 3, 3)" down from top edge on each side.

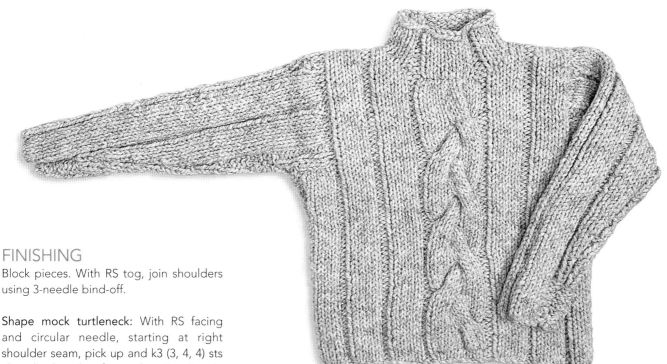

FINISHING

Block pieces. With RS tog, join shoulders using 3-needle bind-off.

Shape mock turtleneck: With RS facing and circular needle, starting at right shoulder seam, pick up and k3 (3, 4, 4) sts along back neck to first purl section, 2 sts in purl section, 7 sts along Cable Panel, 2 sts in purl section, 7 (7, 9, 9) sts along knit section to Front neck, 2 sts in purl section, 7 sts along Front Cable Panel, 2 sts in purl section, 4 (4, 5, 5) sts in knit section to seam—36 (36, 40, 40) sts. Pm for beg of rnd. Rnd 1: K3 (3, 4, 4), p2, k7, p2, k7 (7, 9, 9); p2, k7, p2, k4 (4, 5, 5). Rep Rnd 1 until collar measures 3", bind off loosely in pat. Set in Sleeves. Sew bound-off underarm sts to area above Sleeve markers. Sew under-arm and side seams. Weave in loose ends.

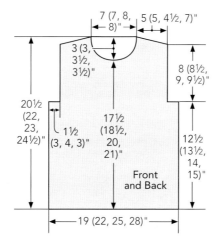

7 (7, 8, 8)"   5 (5, 4½, 7)"

3 (3, 3½, 3½)"

8 (8½, 9, 9½)"

20½ (22, 23, 24½)"

1½ (3, 4, 3)"

17½ (18½, 20, 21)"

12½ (13½, 14, 15)"

Front and Back

19 (22, 25, 28)"

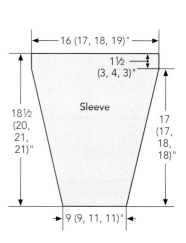

16 (17, 18, 19)"

1½ (3, 4, 3)"

Sleeve

18½ (20, 21, 21)"

17 (17, 18, 18)"

9 (9, 11, 11)"

With large needles, chunky yarn, and a weekend to spare, you can knit a comfortable, casual two-color sweater to wear with a T-shirt and jeans.

DESIGN: LIPP HOLMFELD

SKILL LEVEL: BEGINNER +

color block
PULLOVER

SIZES: S (M, L, XL)

Shown in size M.

When only one number is given, it applies to all sizes. *Note: For ease in working, circle all numbers pertaining to your size.*

FINISHED MEASUREMENTS

Underarm = 38 (42, 45, 48)"

YARNS

Lion Brand Wool-Ease Thick & Quick (Art. 640); 80% acrylic, 20% wool; 3 oz. (86 g); 197 yds. (180 m); super bulky

- 3 (3, 4, 4) balls #149 Charcoal (A)
- 3 (3, 4, 4) balls #099 Fisherman (B)

NEEDLES & EXTRAS

- Size 11 (8 mm) needles OR SIZE NEEDED TO OBTAIN GAUGE
- Size 11 (8 mm) circular needle 29" (used as stitch holder)
- Tapestry needle

GAUGE

10 sts and 16 rows = 4" (10 cm) over pattern stitch. TAKE TIME TO CHECK YOUR GAUGE.

PATTERN STITCH

Row 1 (RS): *K1, p1, rep from * across.
Rows 2 & 4: Purl.
Row 3: *P1, k1, rep from * across.
Rep Rows 1–4 for pat.

Notes: Front and Back are worked half in A and half in B. Always twist the two yarns together at the center on the wrong side by bringing the second yarn up from under the first yarn.
Sleeves are worked from shoulder down.
See page 43 for 3-needle bind-off and ssp.

INSTRUCTIONS
BACK/FRONT (make two)

With A, cast on 24 (26, 28, 30) sts; with B, cast the same number of sts onto the same needle. K the first two rows, remembering to twist A and B tog at the center.
Row 1: Beg pat st. Work even until piece

measures approx 15 (17, 19, 21)", ending with Row 3 of pat. K 4 more rows—16 (18, 20, 22)". Cut both yarn ends, leaving 30" tails. Do not bind off; sl sts to circular needle (cn). Work Front same as Back. Do not cut yarn. **Shape shoulders and Boat Neck:** * With RS tog and using tail from shoulder edge, work 3-needle bind-off across 11 (12, 13, 14) sts, then bind off 13 (14, 15, 16) sts from front side only (this is one side of front boat neck); then bind off 13 (14, 15, 16) front sts with second tail (other side of front boat neck). Turn work and rep from * for other shoulder edge and whole back of boat neck. Cut yarn.

SLEEVES (make two)

Place markers 17½ (18½, 19, 20)" apart centered on the right shoulder seam. With RS facing and A, pick up and k 44 (46, 48, 50) sts between the markers. Work pat for 5 rows, ending with a RS row. **Dec Row:** P1, p2tog, work to last 3 sts, ssp, p1. Cont in pat and work Dec Row every 6th row 7 times more—28 (30, 32, 34) sts rem. Work 4 more rows of pat. K 4 rows. Bind off in k. Make second sleeve with B.

FINISHING

Sew tog side and underarm seams. Weave in all loose ends.

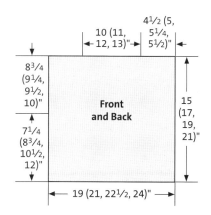

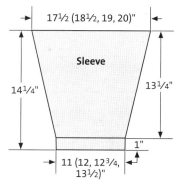

cable & rib
SLEEVELESS SHELL

This stylish sleeveless sweater is a versatile wardrobe accessory. The wishbone cable accent along the front gracefully continues in the mock turtleneck.

DESIGN: MARY MARIK

SKILL LEVEL: BEGINNER+

SIZES: S (M, L, XL, 2X)
Shown in Size S. When only one number is given, it applies to all sizes. *Note: For ease in working, circle all numbers pertaining to your size.*

FINISHED MEASUREMENTS
Underarm = 35 (37, 39, 41, 43)"

YARN
Muench Touch Me (Art. 368); 72% viscose, 28% wool; 1.75 oz. (50 g); 60 yds. (55 m); worsted weight

- 11 (12, 13, 14, 15) balls #3617

NEEDLES & EXTRAS
- Size 6 (4 mm) needles OR SIZE NEEDED TO OBTAIN GAUGE
- Size 6 (4 mm) 16" circular needle OR SIZE NEEDED TO OBTAIN GAUGE
- Cable needle (cn)
- Stitch holders
- Stitch markers
- Tapestry needle

GAUGE
19 sts and 32 rows = 4" (10 cm) over 2×2 Rib. TAKE TIME TO CHECK YOUR GAUGE. *Note: Measure for gauge while slightly stretching the swatch. The gauge is achieved by knitting with a firm tension.*

SPECIAL ABBREVIATIONS
12-st Cable = Sl 3 sts to cable needle (cn) and hold in back of work, k 3 sts through the back loop (tbl), k 3 sts tbl from cn; sl 3 sts to cn and hold in front of work, k 3 sts tbl, k 3 sts tbl from cn.

PATTERN STITCHES
2×2 RIB
Row 1: (RS) K2; *p2, k2; rep from * across.
Row 2: P2; *k2, p2; rep from * across.
Rep Rows 1 and 2 for pat.

WISHBONE CABLE
Rows 1 and 3 (RS): P2, k12 sts tbl, p2.
Row 2 and all WS rows: K2, p12, k2.
Row 5: P2, 12-st Cable, p2.
Row 6: Rep Row 2.

Note: See page 43 for 3-needle bind-off.

INSTRUCTIONS
BACK
Cast on 86 (90, 94, 98, 102) sts. Work in 2×2 Rib for 12 (12½, 12½, 13, 13)", ending with a WS row. **Shape armholes:** Bind off 4 sts in 2×2 Rib at beg of next two rows. **Dec Row:** K1, ssk, work across row until 3 sts rem, k2tog, k1. **Next Row:** P2, work across row until 2 sts rem, p2. Rep these two rows 11 times more—54 (58, 62, 66, 70) sts. Work even until armhole measures 7½ (7½, 8, 8, 8½)", ending with a WS row. Place sts on holder.

FRONT
Cast on 84 (92, 100, 100, 108) sts.
Setup Row (RS): Work 34 (38, 42, 42, 46) sts in 2×2 Rib pat, pm, work 16 sts Wishbone Cable, pm, work 34 (38, 42, 42, 46) sts 2×2 Rib. Work as for Back until armhole measures 5", ending with a WS row. **Shape front neck:** Work 15 (19, 23, 23, 27) sts in Rib, k2tog, k1, work cable, k1, ssk,

work 15 (19, 23, 23, 27) sts in Rib—50 (58, 66, 66, 74) sts.

Next Row (WS): P2, work next 31 (35, 39, 39, 43) sts in pat, place the last 16 sts worked on holder, join 2nd ball of yarn, work in pat to end of row, ending with p2. Working both sides AT THE SAME TIME, dec 1 st at each neck edge every RS row as follows: Work in Rib until 4 sts rem on left front, k2tog, k1, p1. **For other shoulder side:** P1, k1, ssk, work Rib to end of row. Cont decreasing on every RS row 2 (6, 10, 6, 10) times more—15 (15, 15, 19, 19) sts rem each shoulder. Work even until armhole measures 7½ (7½, 8, 8, 8½)". Place shoulder sts on holders.

FINISHING
Join Front to Back at shoulders using 3-needle bind-off.

MOCK TURTLENECK
With RS facing and circular needle, beg at left shoulder seam, pick up and k16 (16, 20, 20, 24) sts along left front neck, work cable pat as est across 16 sts from holder, pick up and k16 (16, 20, 20, 24) sts along right front neck, work rib as est across back neck sts from holder. *Note: Ribbing at back of neck should end with a p1. Pm to mark beg of rnd.* **Next Rnd:** P1; work 16 (16, 20, 20, 24) sts k2, p2 Rib; k12; work p2, k2 Rib to end of rnd, ending p1. Cont working mock turtleneck in 2×2 Rib and Wishbone Cable pats as est for desired height of neckline, remembering to k12 tbl on odd-numbered rnds and k12 on even-numbered rnds for the Wishbone Cable. Bind off loosely in pats as est. Weave in loose ends. *Note: To prevent cable from flaring, during bind-off k2tog over the 12 sts of cable before performing each bind-off.*

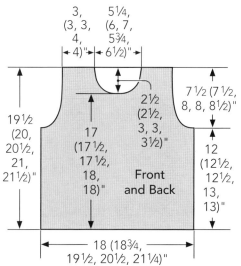

The ladder-and-cable pattern makes this hefty cardigan a fall favorite—one that can easily be adapted for a man's sweater.

DESIGN: KATHY ZIMMERMAN

SKILL LEVEL: INTERMEDIATE

ladders & ropes
CARDIGAN

SIZES: S (M, L, XL, 2X)

Shown in Size M. When only one number is given, it applies to all sizes. *Note: For ease in working, circle all numbers pertaining to your size.*

FINISHED MEASUREMENTS

Underarm = 43½ (45½, 48½, 51, 53½)"

YARN

Lion Brand Kool Wool (Art. 380); 50% merino wool, 50% acrylic; 1.75 oz. (50 g); 60 yds. (55 m); chunky weight

- 20 (21, 23, 25, 27) balls #125 Camel

NEEDLES, BUTTONS & EXTRAS

- Size 9 (5.5 mm) needles
- Size 9 (5.5 mm) 29" circular needle
- Size 10.5 (6.5 mm) needles OR SIZE NEEDED TO OBTAIN GAUGE
- Cable needle (cn)
- Stitch markers
- Tapestry needle
- Five 1" brass shank buttons

GAUGE

13 sts and 18 rows = 4" (10 cm) over Rev St st (p 1 row, k 1 row) using larger needles. 6 sts = 1¾" over Ladder Pattern; 14 sts of Rope Cable = 3¼".
TAKE TIME TO CHECK YOUR GAUGE.

SPECIAL ABBREVIATIONS

2/2 RC = Sl 2 sts to cn and hold in back of work, k2, k2 from cn
2/2 LC = Sl 2 sts to cn and hold in front of work, k2, k2 from cn

PATTERN STITCHES

LADDER—6 sts
Rows 1, 3, 5, 7, 9, and 11 (RS): Knit.
Rows 2, 4, and 12: Purl.
Rows 6, 8, and 10: Knit.
Rep Rows 1–12 for pat.

ROPE CABLE I (Right Cross)—14 sts
Rows 1 and 3 (RS): P2, k1, p2, k4, p2, k1, p2.
Rows 2, 4, and 6: K2, p1, k2, p4, k2, p1, k2.
Row 5: P2, k1, p2, 2/2 RC, p2, k1, p2.
Rep Rows 1–6 for pat.

ROPE CABLE II (Left Cross)—14 sts
Rows 1 and 3 (RS): P2, k1, p2, k4, p2, k1, p2.
Rows 2, 4, and 6: K2, p1, k2, p4, k2, p1, k2.
Row 5: P2, k1, p2, 2/2 LC, p2, k1, p2.
Rep Rows 1–6 for patt.

Note: Sl markers every row. Work all incs and decs one st in from edge.

INSTRUCTIONS
BACK

With smaller needles, cast on 77 (81, 85, 88, 92) sts. K 6 rows, increasing 9 (9, 9, 10, 10) sts evenly spaced on last row, ending on a RS row—86 (90, 94, 98, 102) sts. Change to larger needles.
Foundation Row (WS): K0 (2, 4, 6, 8); *p6, k2, p1, k2, p4, k2, p1, k2; rep from * 3 times; p6, k0 (2, 4, 6, 8).
Setup Row: P0 (2, 4, 6, 8), place marker (pm), * work 6 sts Ladder pat, pm, work 14 sts Rope Cable I, pm, rep from * once, pm; work 6 sts Ladder pat (center back), pm; ** work 14 sts Rope Cable II, pm, work 6 sts Ladder pat, pm; rep from ** once, p0 (2, 4, 6, 8) sts. Work even until piece measures 14½ (15, 15½, 15¾, 16)", ending with a WS row.

Shape armholes: Bind off 8 (8, 9, 10, 11) sts at beg of next 2 rows—70, (74, 76, 78, 80) sts. Work even in pat until armhole measures 8½ (9, 9½, 10, 10½)", ending with a WS row. Shape shoulders and Back neck: Work in pat across 26 (27, 27, 28, 29) sts, join second ball of yarn, bind off center 18 (20, 22, 22, 22) sts for back neck, work across rem 26 (27, 27, 28, 29) sts. Working both sides at once, bind off 2 sts at each neck edge twice, and AT THE SAME TIME, bind off 8 (7, 7, 8, 9) sts at each shoulder edge once, then 7 (8, 8, 8, 8) sts twice—no sts rem.

RIGHT FRONT

With smaller needles, cast on 36 (38, 40, 42, 44) sts. K 6 rows, increasing 5 sts evenly spaced on last row—41 (43, 45, 47, 49) sts. Change to larger needles.
Foundation Row (WS): K0 (2, 4, 6, 8), *p6, k2, p1, k2, p4, k2, p1, k2; rep from * once, pm; k1 (front edge).
Setup Row: K1, *work 14 sts Rope Cable II, pm, work 6 sts Ladder pat, pm, rep from * once, k0 (2, 4, 6, 8) sts. Keeping 1 st in Garter st (k every row) at front edge, work even until piece measures same as Back to armhole shaping, ending with a RS row.

Shape armhole (WS): Bind off 8 (8, 9, 10, 11) sts, work in pat across rem 33 (35, 36, 37, 38) sts, pm at front edge for beg V-neck shaping. V-neck Dec Row (RS): Work in pat until 3 sts rem, k2tog, k1. Rep V-Neck Dec Row at front edge every other row 1 (2, 3, 2, 1) times more, then every 4th row 9 (9, 9, 10, 11) times—22 (23, 23, 24, 25) sts rem. When armhole measures same as back, bind off 8 (7, 7, 8, 9) sts at each shoulder edge once, then 7 (8, 8, 8, 8) sts twice—no sts rem.

LEFT FRONT

With smaller needles, cast on 36 (38, 40, 42, 44) sts. K 6 rows, increasing 5 sts evenly spaced on last row—41 (43, 45, 47, 49) sts. Change to larger needles.
Foundation Row (WS): K1 (front edge), pm; *p6, k2, p1, k2, p4, k2, p1, k2; rep from * once, pm; k0 (2, 4, 6, 8) [Rev St st].
Setup Row: P0 (2, 4, 6, 8) sts , *work 14 sts Rope Cable I, pm, work 6 sts Ladder pat, pm; rep from * once, k1 (front edge). Work to correspond to Right Front, reversing all shaping. V-neck Dec Row (RS): K1, ssk, work in pat to end of row.

SLEEVES (make two)

With smaller needles, cast on 35 (37, 37, 38, 39) sts. K8 rows, increasing 11 (9, 9, 8, 7) sts evenly spaced on last row—46 sts. Change to larger needles.

Foundation Row (WS): *P6, k2, p1, k2, p4, k2, p1, k2; rep from * once, p6.

Setup Row: Work 6 sts Ladder pat, pm, work 14 sts Rope Cable I, pm, work 6 sts Ladder pat (center of sleeve), pm, work 14 sts Rope Cable II, pm, work 6 sts Ladder pat. Cont in pat and inc 1 st at each end every 4th row 0 (4, 9, 14, 19) times, then every 6th row 12 (10, 7, 4, 1) times, incorporating added sts into Rope Cable I at beg of row and into Rope Cable II at end of row on all sizes. **Sizes L and XL ONLY:** Work additional incs after Rope Cables completed in Rev St st on final 2 (4) incs. **Size 2X ONLY:** Work final 6 incs in Ladder pat—70 (74, 78, 82, 86) sts. Work even in pat until piece measures 19¼ (20, 20¾, 21¾, 22¼)". Bind off all sts loosely in pat.

FINISHING

Sew shoulder seams.

Front Bands: With RS facing and circular needle, starting at lower Right Front, pick up and k50 (52, 54, 54, 55) sts along Right Front, pm, pick up and k1 st for V, pm, pick up and k38 (40, 42, 44, 46) sts along Right Front neck, 29 (30, 31, 33, 33) sts along Back neck, 38 (40, 42, 44, 46) sts along Left Front neck, pm, pick up and k 1 st for V, pm, pick up and k50 (52, 54, 54, 55) sts along Left Front—207 (216, 225, 231, 237) sts. **Next Row—Inc. at V (WS):** *P1, k2; rep from *, inc 1 st before and after each V (use markers as guides), end with p1—211, (220, 229, 235, 241) sts. Work 1 row even, working sts as they appear (k1, p2 rib). Mark position of 5 evenly spaced buttonholes on Right Front for woman's version, Left Front for man's. Work yo, k2tog at marked positions on next row. Cont in rib for 3 more rows. Bind off all sts in pat. Sew buttons to button band. Attach sleeves to body. Sew body and sleeve seams. Weave in all ends. Block lightly as needed.

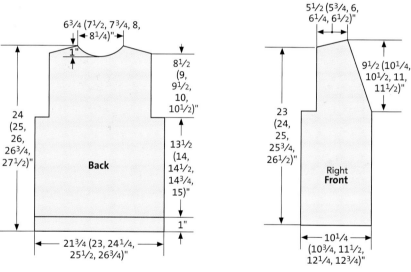

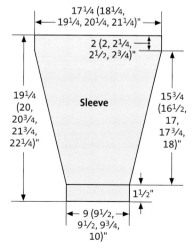

diamond lace
TWIN SET

This twin set segues from the office to evening.
Sizes for the diamonds on the camisole and the cardigan are determined by two different yarn weights.

DESIGN: LILY CHIN

SKILL LEVEL: INTERMEDIATE

CAMISOLE
SIZES: S (M, L, XL, XXL)

Shown in size M. The pattern is written for the smallest size with changes for larger sizes indicated in parentheses. When only one number is given, it applies to all sizes. *Note: For ease in working, before you begin the pattern, circle all numbers pertaining to your size.*

FINISHED MEASUREMENTS

Bust = 35 (38, 41, 44, 47)"
Length = 20½ (21, 21½, 22, 22½)"

YARN

Lion Brand Wool-Ease (Art. 660); 80% acrylic, 20% wool yarn; 435 yds. (400 m); sport weight

- 2 (2, 2, 3, 3) balls #152 Oxford Grey

NEEDLES & EXTRAS

- Size 5 (3.75 mm) knitting needles OR SIZE NEEDED TO OBTAIN GAUGE
- Size 4 (3.5 mm) 16" circular needle
- Stitch markers
- Tapestry needle

GAUGE

20 sts and 28 rows = 4" (10 cm) in Stockinette Stitch (knit 1 row, purl 1 row).
TAKE TIME TO CHECK YOUR GAUGE.

INSTRUCTIONS
BACK

Beg at the lower edge with CIRCULAR needles, cast on 89 (97, 105, 113, 119) sts. Beg Garter st and work for 1". Change to larger needles and St st (k RS rows, p WS rows) working until piece measures approximately 12½" from beg, ending with a WS row. **Shape armholes:** Bind off 5 (6, 7, 8, 8) sts at the beg of next 2 rows, then 0 (3, 4, 4, 4) sts at the beg of next 0 (2, 2, 2, 2) rows. For all sizes, bind off 2 sts at beg of next 2 rows—75 (75, 79, 85, 91) sts. On next RS row, dec 1 st from each end as follows: K2, k2tog, k to within last 4 sts, ssk, k last 2 sts. Rep dec row on next 3 (1, 2, 3, 5) RS rows, then every 4th row 1 (2, 2, 2, 2) time(s). Work even on 65 (67, 69, 73, 75) sts until piece measures approximately 19 (19½, 20, 20½, 21)" from beg, ending with a RS row. **Shape neck:** Purl across first 21 (21, 21, 22, 22) sts, bind off center 23 (25, 27, 29, 31) sts, p remaining sts. Attach another ball of yarn to other side. Working shoulders separately and AT THE SAME TIME, bind off 5 sts from each neck edge once, 3 sts from each neck edge once, and 2 sts from each neck edge 0 (0, 0, 1, 1) times. Dec at neck edge fully fashioned on next RS row as follows: K to within last 4 sts at end of first shoulder, ssk, k last 2 sts; at beg of next shoulder, k2, k2 tog, k to end. Rep this dec row on next 2 (2, 2, 1, 1) RS rows.

Shape shoulders: AT THE SAME TIME, when piece measures approx 20 (20½, 22, 22½, 23)" from beg, end with a WS row. Bind off 4 sts from each shoulder edge once and 3 sts from each shoulder edge twice.

FRONT

Work as for Back, but when piece measures 10 (10½, 11, 11½, 12)" from beg, end with a WS row. Mark off center 15 sts; use stitch markers and sl them as you work. Work Lace Chart A, *page 5*, over these center 15 sts. AT THE SAME TIME, complete piece as for Back, shaping armholes, neck, and shoulders in the same manner.

FINISHING

Block pieces to measurements. Sew shoulder and side seams.

ARMHOLE TRIM

With RS facing, circular needle, and beg at underarm, pick up and k41 (43, 45, 49, 51) sts evenly around each Front and Back armhole—82 (86, 90, 98, 102) sts around. Mark beg of rnd with stitch marker. For Garter st band, work as follows:

Rnd 1: Purl.

Rnd 2: Knit. Rep Rnds 1–2 until Trim measures 1"; bind off.

NECK TRIM

With RS facing, circular needle, and beg at a shoulder, pick up and k53 (55, 57, 59, 61) sts evenly around each Front and Back neck—106 (110, 114, 118, 122) sts. Mark beg of rnd with stitch marker. Work Garter st band as for Armhole Trim, ending after 1"; bind off.

CARDIGAN
SIZES: S (M, L, XL, XXL)

Shown is size M. The pattern is written for the smallest size with changes for larger sizes indicated in parentheses. When only one number is given, it applies to all sizes. *Note: For ease in working, before you begin the pattern, circle all numbers pertaining to your size.*

FINISHED MEASUREMENTS

Bust = 39 (42, 46, 50, 54)"
Length = 23½ (24, 24½, 25, 25½)"

YARN

Lion Brand Wool-Ease (Art. 620); 80% acrylic, 20% wool; 197 yds. (180 m); worsted weight
• 5 (5, 6, 7, 8) balls #152 Oxford Grey

NEEDLES & EXTRAS

• Size 9 (5.5 mm) knitting needles OR SIZE NEEDED TO OBTAIN GAUGE
• Size 8 (5 mm) knitting needles
• Stitch markers
• Tapestry needle

GAUGE

16 sts and 22 rows = 4" (10 cm) over Stockinette stitch (knit 1 row, purl 1 row) using larger needles.
16 sts = 4" (10 cm) over Garter stitch using smaller needles. TAKE TIME TO CHECK YOUR GAUGE.

INSTRUCTIONS
BACK

Beg at lower edge with smaller needles, cast on 80 (86, 94, 102, 110) sts. Beg Garter st and work for 1". Change to larger needles and St st (k RS rows, p WS rows), working until piece measures approx 14½" from beg, ending with a WS row. **Shape armholes:** Bind off 3 (4, 5, 5, 6) sts at beg of next 2 rows. On next RS row, dec 1 st from each end as follows: K2, k2tog, k to within last 4 sts, ssk, k last 2 sts. Rep dec row on next 2 (3, 4, 6, 7) RS rows. Work evenly on 68 (70, 74, 78, 82) sts until piece measures approx 22½ (23, 23½, 24, 24½)" from beg, ending with a RS row.

Shape back neck: Purl across first 24 (24, 25, 27, 28) sts, bind off center 20 (22, 24, 24, 26) sts, purl remaining sts. Attach another ball of yarn to other side. Working shoulders separately and AT THE SAME TIME, bind off 3 (3, 3, 4, 4) sts from each neck edge once for 2 rows, then 2 sts from each neck edge once. **Shape shoulders:** AT THE SAME TIME, after binding off center sts and beg with next RS row, bind off 5 sts from each shoulder edge 3 (3, 3, 3, 2) times. Then bind off 0 (0, 0, 0, 6) sts from each shoulder edge. Bind off rem 4 (4, 5, 6, 6) sts.

RIGHT FRONT

Beg at the lower edge with smaller needles, cast on 39 (41, 45, 49, 53) sts. Beg Garter st and work for 1". Change to larger needles and k across first row for St st, marking off 15 sts after 9th (10th, 11th, 12th, 13th) st from center edge. *Note: Use stitch markers and sl them as you work.* On next RS row, beg Lace Chart B, *page 5*, over these center 15 sts. Continue in St st with the lace panel between markers until piece measures approx 14½" from beg, ending with a RS row. **Shape armholes:** Bind off 3 (4, 5, 5, 6) sts at beg of next row. On next RS row, dec 1 st from armhole edge as follows: Knit to within last 4 sts, ssk, k last 2 sts. Rep dec row on next 2 (3, 4, 6, 7) RS rows. Work even on 33 (33, 35, 37, 39) sts until piece measures approximately 20½ (21, 21½, 22, 22½)" from beg, ending with a WS row.

Shape neck front: Bind off 5 (5, 6, 6, 7) sts at beg of next row, then 3 (3, 3, 4, 4) sts from neck edge, then 2 sts from neck edge. On next RS row, dec 1 st from neck edge as follows: K2, k2tog, k to end. Rep Dec row on next 3 RS rows. **Shape shoulders:** AT THE SAME TIME, when piece measures approx 22½ (23, 23½, 24, 24½)" from beg, shape shoulder as for Back at beg of WS rows.

LEFT FRONT

Work as for Right Front, reversing all shaping as follows: End with a WS row before shaping armholes; end with a RS row before shaping Front neck. Dec at neck edge on RS rows as follows: Knit to within last 4 sts, ssk, k last 2 sts. Shape shoulder at beg of RS rows.

SLEEVES (make two)

Beg at the lower edge with smaller needles, cast on 35 (37, 37, 39, 39) sts. Beg Garter st and work for 1". Change to larger needles and St st, marking off center 15 sts. Work Lace Chart A over these center 15 sts after 2 rows of St st, beg on RS row. AT THE SAME TIME, inc 1 st each end after first 2 and before last 2 sts every other row 0 (0, 0, 0, 5) times, every 4th row 0 (3, 12, 18, 16) times, then every 6th row 15 (13, 6, 1, 0) times. Work even on 65 (69, 73, 77, 81) sts until Sleeve measures approx 20 (19½, 18, 17, 16)" from beg, ending with a WS row.

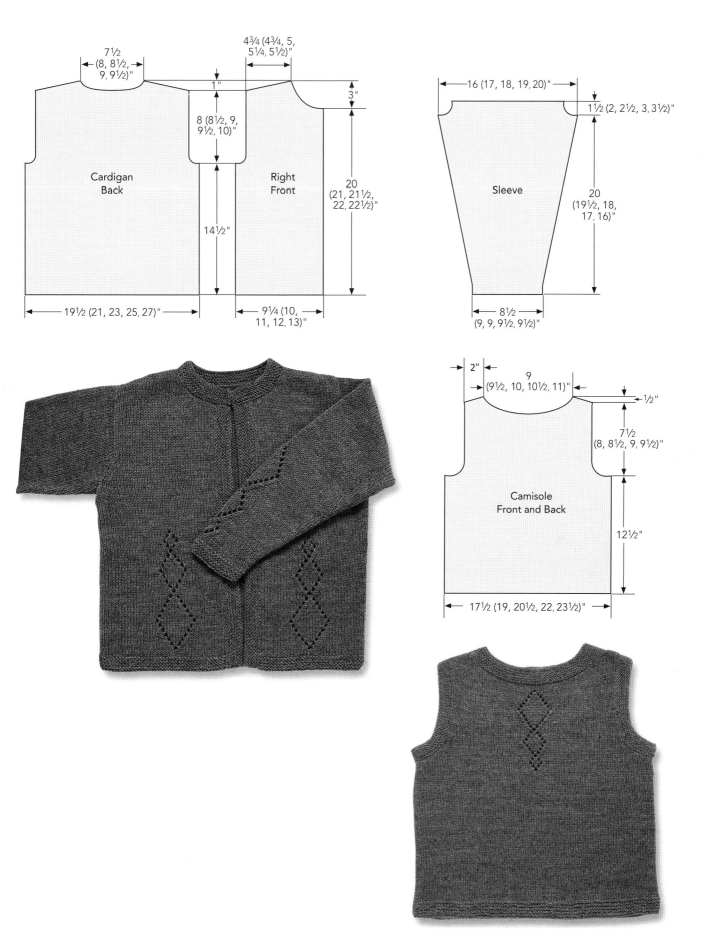

7½
(8, 8½,
9, 9½)"

4¾ (4¾, 5,
5¼, 5½)"

1"

3"

8 (8½, 9,
9½, 10)"

Cardigan
Back

Right
Front

14½"

20
(21, 21½,
22, 22½)"

19½ (21, 23, 25, 27)"

9¼ (10,
11, 12, 13)"

16 (17, 18, 19, 20)"

1½ (2, 2½, 3, 3½)"

Sleeve

20
(19½, 18,
17, 16)"

8½
(9, 9, 9½, 9½)"

2"

9
(9½, 10, 10½, 11)"

½"

7½
(8, 8½, 9, 9½)"

Camisole
Front and Back

12½"

17½ (19, 20½, 22, 23½)"

Shape sleeve caps: Bind off 3 (4, 5, 5, 6) sts beg next 2 rows. On next RS row, dec 1 st from each end as follows: K2, k2tog, k to within last 4 sts, ssk, k last 2 sts. Rep Dec row on next 2 (3, 4, 6, 7) RS rows. Bind off rem 53 sts on next RS row.

FINISHING

Block pieces to measurements. Sew shoulder seams. Set in sleeves. Sew side and sleeve seams.

RIGHT FRONT TRIM

With RS facing and smaller needles and beg at lower edge, pick up and k86 (88, 90, 92, 94) sts evenly spaced to top of neck. Work Garter st (knit every row) for 1"; bind off.

LEFT FRONT TRIM

With RS facing, smaller needles, and beg at top of neck edge, pick up and k86 (88, 90, 92, 94) sts evenly spaced to bottom. Work Garter st (knit every row) for 1"; bind off.

NECK TRIM

With RS facing and smaller needles, beg at side edge of Right Front Trim. Pick up and k24 (25, 26, 27, 28) sts evenly to shoulder, 28 (30, 32, 34, 36) sts evenly along back neck, and 24 (25, 26, 27, 28) sts evenly to Left Front neck edge. Work Garter st (knit every row) on 76 (80, 84, 88, 92) sts for 1"; bind off.

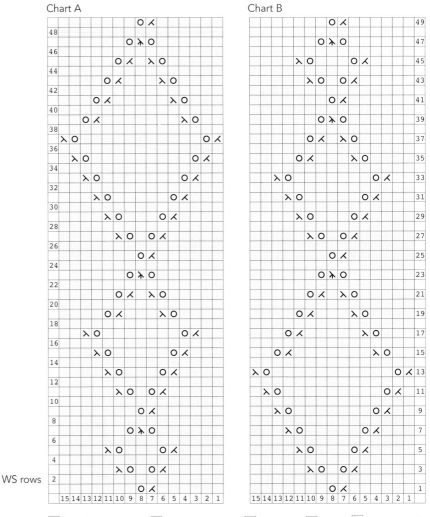

Chart A Chart B

☐ k on RS, p on WS Ⓞ yarn over or yo ⋌ k 2 tog ⋋ ssk ⋏ slip one, k 2 tog, pass slipped st over

basics of cable formation

Most rows of cable knitting involve simply working stitches as they are arranged on previous rows—"knit the knits and purl the purls." The excitement comes on the crossing rows, when the stitches are knit out of order.

Simple cables may appear to rotate to the left or to the right. Holding stitches on the cable needle to the back while the next knit stitches are worked makes Right-Crossing Cables (also called Back Cables). (See photographs 1–3, *below*.)

Holding the cable needle and its stitches to the front while the next knit stitches are worked makes Left-Crossing Cables (also called Front Cables). (See photographs 4–6, *below*.) Cables that appear to be braided are a combination of left- and right-crosses.

Most often, cables are worked in stockinette stitch against a background of reverse stockinette stitch or seed stitch. These textured backgrounds add depth to the design and focus attention on the cable. Cables may even appear to lie separately on the background. A stitch dictionary is a great place to find a collection of cables to knit.

following instructions in words and symbols

There are many cable variations, and although there is no standard description for executing a cable, many explanations are quite similar. Always check the instructions for specific abbreviations and terms that are used in your pattern. Photocopying the abbreviations guide so that you can easily refer to it while you work is also helpful.

Some patterns will have a text-only version of instructions, and others will have charted instructions in which each box of the graph represents a stitch. A chart includes symbols representing the cable techniques used. A stitch key is provided to explain the symbols for all stitches including the cables. Symbols usually mimic the stitch they represent; the chart will give you an idea how the pattern will look after it is knit.

Read the charts from bottom to top and from right to left for right-side rows and from left to right for wrong-side rows. Most charts have numbers along one side. Begin at Row 1, indicated either on the left or the right side of the chart.

After you've worked a few repeats of the entire cable pattern, you may be able to "read" the cable and anticipate future crossing rows. This frees you from having to rely on the instructions row by row, but you'll still want to check the chart occasionally.

tips for making cables

● Pay special attention to gauge. Follow the pattern instructions for measuring gauge. The more cables on a piece and the more times they cross one another, the more the fabric will pull in. Never assume that the Stockinette stitch gauge and the gauge over cables are the same, for they can be dramatically different.

● If you decide to add cables to an otherwise plain sweater, keep in mind that cables use more yarn than a smoother pattern stitch, so you must plan accordingly.

● If the bound-off edge is several rows beyond a crossing row, the fabric may become distorted and difficult to seam. You can minimize the distortion by binding off a row or two after the cable-crossing stitches.

● When you are a cable novice, start with a simple project before you move on to a more complex design. Choose a garment with one cable or several cables that are identical.

● Ignore your "mistakes" as they can become a creative new stitch pattern and add a one-of-a-kind element to your work.

● Cables are an essential element in your knitting repertoire. You'll be surprised how much fun they can be once you've practiced making them.

knitting basics

Abbreviations

beg	begin(ning)(s)
CC	contrasting color
cn	cable needle
cont	continue(d) (ing)
C4F	cable 4 front
dec	decrease
dpn	double-pointed needle(s)
est	established
inc	increase
k or K	knit
k2tog	knit 2 together
knitwise or kwise	insert needle into stitch as if to knit
M1	make 1 stitch
MC	main color
p or P	purl
pat	pattern
PM or pm	place marker
psso	pass the slipped stitch over
p2sso	pass 2 slipped stitches over
purlwise or pwise	insert needle into stitch as if to purl
rem	remain(ing) (s)
rep	repeat
rnd(s)	round(s)
rep	repeat
RS	right side(s)
sl	slip
sl1k	slip 1 knitwise
sl1p	slip 1 purlwise
st(s)	stitch(es)
St st	Stockinette stitch
skp	slip, knit, pass over
ssk	slip, slip, knit
ssp	slip, slip, purl
p2tog	purl 2 together
tog	together
WS	wrong side(s)
yf	yarn forward
yib or ytb	yarn in back or yarn to back of work
yif or ytf	yarn in front or yarn to front of work
yo	yarn over

cable cast-on

step 1

Make a slipknot on the left needle.

step 2

Working into the loop of the knot, knit a stitch; transfer it to the left needle.

step 3

Insert right needle between the last two stitches. Knit a stitch and transfer it to left needle. Repeat this step for each additional stitch.

knit stitch

step 1

Insert the right-hand needle from front to back into the first stitch on the left-hand needle. Notice that the right-hand needle is behind the left-hand needle.

step 2
Form a loop by wrapping the yarn under and around the right-hand needle.

step 3
Pull the loop through the stitch so the loop is in front of the work.

step 4
Slip the first or "old" knit stitch over and off the tip of the left-hand needle.

purl stitch

step 1
With your yarn in front of the work, put the right-hand needle from back to front into the first stitch on the left-hand needle.

step 2
Form a loop by wrapping the yarn on top of and around the right-hand needle.

step 3
Pull the loop through the stitch to make a new purl stitch.

step 4
Slip the first or "old" purl stitch over and off the tip of the left-hand needle.

p1b
Purl through the back loop.

m1 (make 1 stitch)
Work an increase by lifting the horizontal thread lying between the needles and placing it onto the left needle. Work the new stitch through the back loop.

decreasing stitches
Following are three decrease stitches. When possible, work increases and decreases on the right side of the work. The instructions below will help when you make paired decreases (as on a sleeve or sweater front or back), where one slants to the right and one slants to the left. Your decreases should always match the shaping of the piece.

k2tog
Knit two together (decreased stitch slants to the right). Working from left to right, insert the top of the right-hand needle into the second, then the first stitch on the left-hand needle and knit the two stitches together.

p2tog
Purl two together (decreased stitch slants to the right). Working from right to left, insert the tip of the right-hand needle into the first two stitches on the left-hand needle and purl the two stitches together.

ssk
Decreased stitch slants to the left. Slip next two stitches to right needle singly and knitwise, insert tip of left needle through front loop of both stitches, and knit them together.

3-needle bind-off
With RSs together, hold in one hand two needles with an equal number of stitches on each and with points going in same direction. Using a third needle of the same size, knit together one stitch from each needle. * Knit together next stitch from each needle, pass first stitch worked over second to bind off; rep from * across to bind off all stitches.

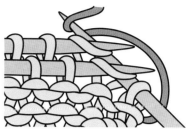

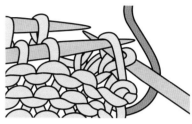

grafting stockinette stitch together
Hold wrong sides together with the needles pointed to the right. Thread yarn tail into yarn needle. * Insert needle knitwise through the first stitch on front needle and let the stitch drop from the needle. Insert needle into the second stitch on front needle purlwise and pull yarn through, leaving the stitch on the needle. Insert needle into the first stitch on the back needle purlwise and let it drop from the needle. Insert needle knitwise through second stitch on the back needle and pull the yarn through, leaving the stitch on the needle. Repeat from * across until all stitches have been joined. Adjust tension as necessary. Weave in loose ends.

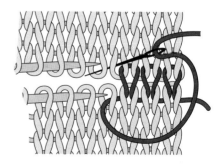

Better Homes and Gardens®
Creative Collection™

Editorial Director
Gayle Goodson Butler

Editor-in-Chief
Beverly Rivers

Executive Editor   Karman Wittry Hotchkiss

Editorial Manager   **Art Director**
Ann Blevins   Brenda Drake Lesch

Copy Chief   Mary Heaton
Administrative Assistant   Lori Eggers
Contributing Editor   Margaret Smith
Contributing Graphic Designer   Tracy S. Devenney
Contributing Copy Editor   Pegi Bevins
Contributing Proofreader   Laura Collins

Senior Vice President
Bob Mate

Vice President, Publishing Director
William R. Reed

Group Publisher   Stephen B. Levinson
Group Marketing Director   Cathy E. Smith
General Manager   Tom Harty
Senior Marketing Manager   Suzy Johnson

Publishing Group President
Jack Griffin

Chairman and CEO   William T. Kerr
President and COO   Stephen M. Lacy

In Memoriam
E. T. Meredith III (1933–2003)